T0148790

Conserving Liberty

The Hoover Institution gratefully acknowledges
the following individuals and foundations
for their significant support of the
Boyd and Jill Smith Task Force
on Virtues of a Free Society
and this publication:

BOYD AND JILL SMITH

WILLIAM E. SIMON FOUNDATION

Conserving Liberty

MARK BLITZ

HOOVER INSTITUTION PRESS
STANFORD UNIVERSITY   STANFORD, CALIFORNIA

The Hoover Institution on War, Revolution and Peace, founded at Stanford University in 1919 by Herbert Hoover, who went on to become the thirty-first president of the United States, is an interdisciplinary research center for advanced study on domestic and international affairs. The views expressed in its publications are entirely those of the authors and do not necessarily reflect the views of the staff, officers, or Board of Overseers of the Hoover Institution.

www.hoover.org

Hoover Institution Press Publication No. 617

Hoover Institution at Leland Stanford Junior University,
Stanford, California 94305-6010

First printing 2011
17 16 15 14 13 12 11   7 6 5 4 3 2 1

Manufactured in the United States of America

The paper used in this publication meets the minimum
Requirements of the American National Standard for
Information Sciences—Permanence of Paper for Printed
Library Materials, ANSI/NISO Z39.48-1992. ♾

Cataloging-in-Publication Data is available from
the Library of Congress.
ISBN-13: 978-0-8179-1424-0 (cloth. : alk. paper)
ISBN-13: 978-0-8179-1426-4 (e-book)

To Ellen and our Family

*The permanent things in life tend somehow to surprise us
more than the great changes we see around us.*

—Margaret Thatcher
Speech on investiture as Chancellor of
The College of William & Mary,
February 5, 1994

CONTENTS

FOREWORD

The Hoover Institution's Boyd and Jill Smith Task Force on the Virtues of a Free Society aims to clarify the beliefs, practices, and institutions that play a crucial role in forming and sustaining liberty, and a distinctly American way of life. By examining the political thought and culture of the American founding, the historical evolution of government and society, and changing public opinion, the group will reflect on the fabric of our civil society. The membership of the task force includes cochairs Peter Berkowitz and David Brady, along with Gerard V. Bradley, James W. Ceaser, William Damon, Robert P. George, Tod Lindberg, Harvey C. Mansfield, Russell Muirhead, Clifford Orwin, and Diana Schaub.

Contributing to the task force efforts, Mark Blitz has written *Conserving Liberty*, which addresses the elements of individual liberty and freedom as the core of American conservatism's strength. In so doing, he focuses on preserving natural rights, on responsibility and other virtues, and on promoting individual excellence and self-government.

John Raisian
Tad and Dianne Taube Director
Hoover Institution, Stanford University

PREFACE

The immediate impetus for this book was a series of discussions at the Hoover Institution in which I participated in 2009 and 2010. The discussions were held under the auspices of the Boyd and Jill Smith Task Force on Virtues of a Free Society. The other participants are welcome to take credit for whatever in the book seems reasonable to them. I also wish to thank my research assistants at Claremont McKenna College's Henry Salvatori Center for the Study of Individual Freedom, Aditya Bindal, Laura Sucheski, and Elizabeth Van Buskirk.

Mark Blitz
Claremont, California
April, 2011

INTRODUCTION:
THE IMPORTANCE OF
CONSERVATISM

I intend in this book to clarify and defend contemporary American conservatism. Conservatism's future is especially significant because it has become the name for the political views that support liberty, good character, strong families, the worth of religion, economic growth, limited government, and vigorous national defense. It is important to understand it correctly, therefore, not primarily as one movement vs. another—"conservatives" vs. "liberals"—but because (at its best) it seeks to conserve our country's core principles, practices, and institutions.

These principles should be common ground on which both conservatives and liberals rest, not the monopoly of one. Indeed, the most common name for our core is not conservatism, but liberal democracy.[1] Nonetheless, today's liberals or "progressives" depart from liberal democratic

1

standards more often, more broadly, and more profoundly than do today's conservatives.

It is foolish to expect our way of life to survive without strong action to defend it and good education to explain it. Political health is not automatic but requires judgment and choice. The passive and foolish are prey to the determined and clever. Although it is obvious that books do not act, they can help teach. I wish to contribute to our understanding by illuminating and in this way helping to conserve our principles. The prognosis is poor if we understand conservatism incorrectly. It is also poor unless liberalism reestablishes itself unashamedly on our country's basic principles. I hope to contribute to this effort too.

Conservatism and the Fear of Decline

After conservatives lost the 2008 elections they worried that their ideas were no longer appealing. Events soon showed their political concern to be excessive, but their immediate fear was replaced by something deeper. Sensible people now worry about our country's overall direction. What recently seemed to be merely a slow decline looks to some as a steady and even headlong slide. This sense of crisis is exacerbated for many by the Obama administration's actions, but is not simply caused by them. Extraordinary budget deficits and a sputtering economy, mandates to redistribute wealth and favor politically connected groups and companies, illegal and unmanaged immigration, declining rates of legitimate childbirths and expanding illegitimacy, increasing, unavoidable, vulgarity and decreasing intellectual and artistic seriousness, uncontrolled technology and unconstrained judges—all this leads people to believe that we direct less and less of our lives. The legal, scientific, and cultural milieu of our actions seems to move dangerously and relentlessly beyond anyone's control. More fundamentally, the love and understanding of freedom that shaped the country appear to motivate fewer and fewer Americans. Self-government seems more rhetoric than reality when we are urged to share every dollar, encouraged to watch every word, and expected to acknowledge every bureaucrat's uncanny wisdom.

This sense of decline is felt most deeply and expressed most ably by conservatives. It is from them that immediate challenges to our descent occur politically. And it is by them that the intellectual crisis at the root of our decline must be challenged. Many narrow or mistaken views of American conservatism exist; several arose from friends and foes after the 2008 election. We should reject what is wrong in these views. American conservatism does not mean preserving forever the mistakes that others have made. It means conserving and enlivening the fundamental grounds on which we are based. It defers to reasonable principles, not to fleeting decisions. It is therefore radical, not passive. But, in defending conservatism we should also acknowledge and confront its genuine limits and not dream them away.

Conservatism and Freedom

The heart of American principles is our emphasis on individual liberty rather than on history or tradition. This is the true importance and value of contemporary American conservatism. As Ronald Reagan wrote before he became President, "the basis of conservatism is a desire for . . . more individual freedom."[2] I will therefore use the first chapter of my book to sketch the elements of conservatism that appeal to individuals, as we value our own liberty. Reminding people to consider ourselves first of all as free individuals and not in group, class, racial, or gender terms is the heart of American conservatism's strength.

This may seem to be an obvious, inevitable, or unchallenged appeal. But one might appeal instead to group identities— to religious, ethnic, national, or gender solidarity. One might suggest to people that they conceive themselves primarily in these collective ways, or conceive others this way. One might especially ask governments to think in terms of groups, or have people think collectively about their own relation to government.

These group conceptions are not mere abstractions but have been powerful historically. Most of them precede individualism. People normally act as if they are so embedded in their groups that "I" makes sense only within such "we's."

In our time, affirmative action, radical feminism, and widespread income-redistribution have corrupted the sound self-reliance and individualism that we once took for granted. We have produced a world comparable in its social distortions to the economic distortions produced by the overregulation that came to a head during Jimmy Carter's presidency. Indeed, these policies of group-allocation are grounded largely in the intellectual turn that considers equality more to require the redistribution of income than the assertion of rights, and fairness more to require group preference than equal opportunity. It is not people's interests and passions alone, but, rather, these matters as formed by opinion and, finally, opinion as directed by the intellect that guides our politics. One intellectual issue we face today is that thinking in terms of group action and rewards distorts a true understanding of individual freedom and rights. To recapture our future we must conserve our origin. As during the Reagan era, the backward glance must produce the cutting edge.

The historical dominance of classes and groups affects conservatives as well as liberals. It is not only contemporary liberalism's affirmative action, gender politics, and ethnic spoils and sensitivities that affirm such groups. Conservatives, too, often celebrate them and the activities that depend on them. In fact, the "traditional" European conservatism that I will soon discuss is grounded in groups, although historically, not ideologically. Today's conservatives, moreover, not liberals, have led our most recent religious renaissance, defended women's special love of family and boys' special energy on the schoolyard, and gazed longingly toward small communities and one's steady place in their practices and traditions. Each of these efforts looks more to facts of membership than it does to individuals as such.

The merits of some of these standpoints seem clear, and their tension with individual freedom is visible. Nonetheless, individual liberty is the most powerful, reliable, and true standpoint from which to clarify and secure conservatism.

It is naturally and reasonably defensible, if not always recognized. It appeals to justifiable equality. It protects the freedom that much current group-talk restricts. And, it can allow us to deal thoughtfully with the importance of differences among groups, genders, and communities. This suggests, of course, that the individual standpoint I will defend differs from libertarian excess.

Conservatism and Virtue

Individual freedom alone cannot produce happiness. We also need good character. Conservatism that supports liberty requires a significant measure of ethical excellence. It is not neutral or indifferent. I will argue that contemporary conservatism helps to advance character because it requires certain virtues. Part of my discussion and defense of conservatism will therefore involve connecting liberty to virtue. This will also help to meet some typical objections to conservatism and consider ways that liberty itself contributes to what ails contemporary life. The argument that conservatism is disreputable because it favors naked self-interest is false, because virtue helps others as well as oneself. Similarly incorrect is the view that conservatism is unjust because it is selfishly inegalitarian. For, conservatism defends equal rights.

I will begin my analysis of conservatism and virtue (in the second chapter) by showing that we need certain virtues to secure our rights and use them successfully. Although this need helps to promote their presence, it does not guarantee it. Chief among these virtues, as American statesmen from the founders to contemporary presidents have said, is responsibility. "We arrived at this point," President Obama tells us in the introductory message to his first budget, *A New Era of Responsibility*, "as a result of an era of profound irresponsibility that engulfed both private and public institutions. . . . And we can bring about a new sense of responsibility among Americans from every walk of life and from every corner of the country."[3] To grasp conservatism's merits we must understand the substance of responsibility, toleration, and other virtues.

Conservatism and Excellence

Liberty, virtue, and excellence cannot flourish apart from the stable expectations that families, conventions, traditions, and institutions nourish. In order to thrive, these institutions require authority that we cannot question at each and every turn. Individual liberty, however, often challenges stable expectations and authority, just as it counters thinking in terms of groups. How, then, can we show that a regime of liberty is not ultimately self-defeating? I will begin my third chapter by indicating how institutional authority works, why it is necessary, and where it supports the intellectually and morally excellent. I intend to clarify how natural rights and their associated virtues can be a base from which to secure and preserve necessary institutions. But I will not pretend that the conflict between the radicalism of liberty and the stability of authority is unreal.

Intellectuals often criticize democracies for their intellectual and cultural mediocrity and vulgarity. This objection has been standard for at least two hundred years. High "culture" is assailed by the vulgarity of the low. As Walter Berns suggests, however, "what began in nineteenth century Britain as a serious critique of the new liberal democracy," evolved for many into a merely fashionable and political attack. It "became in contemporary America" simply "a contemptuous 'bourgeois-bashing.'"[4]

Conservatives are especially criticized by today's liberals for irrationality, by which the critics mean what for them is religious excess. We are treated regularly to the spectacle of vapid celebrities pretending to fear the emergence of American theocracy. "The fear of theocracy," Ross Douthat remarks in *First Things*

> has become a defining panic of the Bush era, reaching a fever pitch in the weeks after the 2004 election. . . . The movement of religious voters into the GOP played a role in Bush's victory, but the uptick in his support between 2000 and 2004 seems mainly to have reflected national-security concerns. Still, these pesky facts didn't stop Garry Wills from announcing the end of the Enlightenment and the arrival of jihad in America, or Jane Smiley from bemoaning the "ignorance and bloodlust" of Bush voters in thrall to a fire-and-brimstone God, or left-wing bloggers from chattering about "Jesusland" and "fundies" and plotting their escape to Canada.[5]

In my third chapter, I will also explore these charges, and develop conservatives' reasonable responses to them. After all, it is conservatives more than liberals who protect the Great Books of Western Civilization and rigorous education that attends to merit. Conservatism requires intelligent attention to what is good.

Conservatism and Self-Government

The standpoint of liberty raises questions about government's scope. Small government, limited government, government that stays off people's backs are conservative watchwords. Examples of government's foolishness, excess, and incompetence give conservatives bitter delight. I will discuss government first by examining self-governing as a site of freedom and virtue, and then by sketching broad standards for sensible law and policy. I will keep in mind conservatism's caution or modesty, and its preference for private mechanisms whenever common action proves necessary. I will conclude by exploring how free citizens might best use and control expert advice and technology generally.

Conservatism and Tradition

Conservatism grounded in individual liberty differs from the traditional or European conservatism that some intellectuals have in mind when they discuss conservatism and criticize it. This older conservatism wished to conserve the stability, traditions, and practices that it believed characterized the life that the French Revolution tried so drastically to overturn. Perhaps, indeed, it sought to restore not a true but a beautified or romanticized picture of these traditions. Whatever the merits of some traditional practices, the world many European conservatives defended was at peace with inherited class distinctions, a low, fixed, or largely stable standard of living, and the dominance of agriculture over manufacturing. To identify American conservatism with such conservatism is therefore to condemn it as alien, inegalitarian, irrational (because focused on tradition as such), and backward rather than progressive. Because these qualities are unpopular, American conservatism's enemies wish to saddle it with them, even if they admire or pretend to admire some of its elements. If the only honest conservative is one in this European style, he will be a perpetual loser in American elections. "Conservatism" would forever be the doctrine of the privileged and parasitical.

The basic element common to European conservatism and today's American conservatism or, indeed, any conservatism is its wish to conserve. One should see, however, that not every conservative must wish to secure only those practices admired by early nineteenth-century or other traditionalists. The United States was founded on revolutionary principles of equal liberty, so what we wish to conserve differs from European tradition. What we seek to preserve is more individual, rational, egalitarian, and industrial than is the *ancien régime*. A still more ancient "conservatism," moreover, the kind one finds in Aristotle's political works, attempts primarily to secure neither individual rights nor local religious and economic practices. Its aim, rather, is to secure the virtues of character that embody what is rational in human happiness. Ultimately, one cannot judge any "conserving" to be good without evaluating what it seeks to conserve. The good American conservative is not one who feels duty-bound to maintain every law and practice that contemporary liberals produce.

Although conservatism's worth depends on its substance, there is often something useful in the old as old, or the familiar as familiar, namely, stability, safety, predictability, and modesty. These provide the boundaries that we use to direct and focus our activities. No one is free to enjoy the fruits of his labor or the pleasures of his leisure in a continually tumultuous environment. Respect for familiar practices and ways, moreover, can often elevate the irrationalities and necessities of one's given world into something sensible and coherent.

This cautious element of conservatism protects the good sense embodied in customary practices from what is arbitrary, idiosyncratic, and tyrannical. It defends prudent care, not willful boldness. It is this factor that fits with "conservative" dispositions individually, modest expectations about whether "improvements" truly improve, and caution about the possibilities of perfection and the malleability of people.

It is nonetheless reasonable to ask whether merely to defend the familiar is not often in effect to protect unjustified privilege, unnecessary irrationality, and squalid poverty. It is sensible to worry that caution might become passivity. How far and for how long must talent at the bottom modestly accept crumbs from fraud at the top? In the last analysis, we must justify and dignify the security of the stable by the merit of what it secures. Even what is desirable about the familiar needs to be discussed in more universal terms, such as the ones—stability, coherence, and respect—I just sketched. The choiceworthiness of the ordinary should find its place within the excellence of the rational. American conservatism reveres natural rights that we can defend rationally and venerates a Constitution produced by the conscious design to secure these rights. The attraction of American conservatism is its remarkably successful attempt to unite the stability of what we accept with practices that stem from a reasoned understanding of what is good. A liberty whose grounds and conditions are misunderstood weakens the longevity and authority that conservatives prize.

CHAPTER ONE

Conserving Natural Rights

I concluded the introduction by suggesting that American conservatism successfully unites the security of accepted practices with a reasoned understanding of what is good. The Constitution is meant to be revered, but it is also revolutionary. Our tradition is composed primarily of liberal democratic or constitutional teachings, institutions, and practices.

A central cause of our political mistakes is the failure to understand our origin. Vague pronouncements about freedom, intellectual pabulum about the founders, and distorting principles so they seem to accord with selfish interests are endemic. By passing President Obama's health care legislation, Nancy Pelosi told the world during the concluding House debate about the bill on March 21, 2010:

we will honor the vows of our founders who in the Declaration of Independence said that we are 'endowed by our Creator with certain unalienable rights, that among these are life, liberty and the pursuit of happiness.' This legislation will lead to healthier lives, more liberty to pursue hopes and dreams and happiness for the American people. This is an American proposal that honors the traditions of our country.[1]

This is but one of countless examples. It is a wonder that our roots have not altogether decayed in their decades-long bath of acidic babble and mush. To be worthy of success, genuine conservatism must recover the true bearing and intention of our beginning.

The central American conservative principle, and the one most attractive politically, is liberty, or freedom. Our founding document is the Declaration of Independence. Unless we attempt to understand and conserve its principles, we cannot truly be conserving what is most native to us, and what is most our own. As Speaker Pelosi only partially reminded us on her stumbling journey toward "progress:"

> We hold these truths to be self-evident: That all men are created equal; that they are endowed by their Creator with certain unalienable rights; that among these are life, liberty and the pursuit of happiness; that, to secure these rights, governments are instituted among men, deriving their just powers from the consent of the governed. . . .

It is the "laws of nature and of nature's God" that "entitle" us to a "separate and equal station" "among the powers of the earth."

Rights

The Declaration of Independence announces inalienable individual rights. Because natural rights are our tradition we come to take them for granted, practically and intellectually. What, however, is a right? Rights are often misunderstood, which obscures their meaning and why they are desirable. A related mistake is the implicit view that however we understand rights and liberty they are mere preferences with no ground.

If we explore rights more fully we will see that they do rest on solid ground. Our foundation is not arbitrary or accidental. A right is an authority to reflect, prefer, choose, use, proceed, and act that we justly possess. As an authority, it is not a mere privilege or opportunity. As an authority to reflect, prefer, choose, use, proceed, and act, a right is freedom of self-direction, not a particular outcome or a bare state of being unobstructed. As justly possessed or deserved, a right is not something stolen or usurped. An inalienable right is an authority one cannot give up, unlike a fleeting possession. It is not something one keeps only at another's sufferance. The individual natural rights with which we are endowed, therefore, are individual authorities to reflect, prefer, choose, use, proceed, and act that always belong to us.

It is easy to confuse such rights with rights as procedures, or good things that others should guarantee or give to me. We believe we have rights to a fair trial, sympathetic jurors, safe roads, fast cars, good education, useful degrees, fine medical care, gourmet food, equal treatment, compassionate treatment, decent incomes, premium seats, fat settlements from misbehaving corporations, and never-ending growth and plenty. These often contradictory "rights," however, differ from the individual rights at our foundation. Our founding rights are authorities to reflect, prefer, choose, use, proceed, and act, not particular procedures, outcomes, and goods. The similarity is that in all these cases we believe "rights" to be what we justly, properly, or "righteously" deserve. The similarity in a few of these cases—the right to a fair trial, for example—is that some flow from natural rights once we try to secure these in self-governing political communities. But, again, the difference in all cases is that only individual natural rights are inalienable authorities for self-direction. They therefore fit together with free action and effort, but do not assure accomplishment and success.

It is easy enough to see why we supplement and piece by piece replace our understanding of individual rights with the notion that rights are deserved outcomes that someone—the government, the wealthy, magical providers—should guarantee. The discipline of individual freedom can be difficult and its outcome not assured.[2] Necessary imperfection means that even the best government's protection of rights falls short of justice. Bad luck leads to unfairness. The wealthy seek and often find ways to perpetuate their advantages. Especially when growth is not robust, the economic rewards of liberty are insufficiently widespread. In a regime grounded on rights, where rights among other things mean what one deserves, dissatisfaction with the results of pursuing individual natural rights may lead to calls for "rights" that are merely the outcomes one desires. All good words become hollowed so that we can stuff them with the comfortable and familiar. *"Rights"* are no exception.

This general possibility of misunderstanding rights, however, is insufficient to explain all that actually takes place in substituting rights as outcomes for rights as natural authorities. Why do we claim *these* misunderstood "rights?" One reason is that the two centuries of political and philosophical thought that follow America's founding argue against the truth of individual rights. They claim, instead, that we are formed primarily by social, economic, class, and historical forces and must find our happiness within what they give. Not everyone makes such arguments, but this is the dominant trend.[3] Indeed, it is a trend that forms and to a degree is begun by conservative writers, as traditionally understood.

One might even fear from these trends that the arguments against individual rights (or "bourgeois rights," as the Marxists say), could become so widespread that defending rights would fade altogether. This would be wrong. Rights are so ingrained in our politics and law that they are and were more likely to be misinterpreted than jettisoned. Several of the thinkers who began the movement away from natural rights, such as Kant and Hegel, nonetheless incorporated them in their thought. Battles against the Nazis and Communists made evident that individual liberty was a core of what we were defending. And, the natural power of individual rights means that they make their presence felt whenever circumstances are at all reasonable.

The theoretical turn away from individual rights is in any event insufficient to explain fully the new confusion about what they are. Intellectual and political events may interact, but they do not determine each other. In the United States, the theoretical change influenced journalists and academics, who then began to develop the political opinions we summarize as "progressivism." These views helped to form the policies of Wilson and the two Roosevelts. Political opinions alone, however, do not cause policy. Actual events need to be addressed. The closing of the frontier, the expansion of large cities, the growth of industry, the rise of monopolies, and the increasing dependence of Americans on jobs provided by someone else all produced significant difficulties.

Whether government needed to meet these challenges as it did one hundred years ago, or could have accommodated them less intrusively is another matter. Many conservatives doubt the wisdom of government's growth under Wilson and Theodore Roosevelt, just as many doubt that the New Deal responded to the depression effectively. Others concede that economic complexity, lack of timely consumer information about sophisticated products, and dangers to health and safety justified some growth in government. Ronald Reagan, for example, objected primarily to domestic programs that began under Lyndon Johnson in the 1960s, and to irresponsible prosecution of the Cold War.[4]

Government growth combined with opinions that see us more as members of groups than as individuals to create a view of rights as goods that others ought to give us. Rights increasingly lost their meaning as justified authorities to engage in one's own efforts and enjoy the fruits (and suffer the shortcomings) of one's own actions. The new view grew during the 1960s when the civil rights movement joined

Johnson's Great Society. It is especially visible in programs of affirmative action. Demands, often successful demands, for unequal treatment were increasingly advanced as one's right without even being justified by the unique circumstance of the horror of slavery. The original sense of individual rights became buried under the weight of group claims to redress and, in time, to advantage. Much of the conservative revival in the United States that issued in Reagan's election and the Reagan era received its energy from revulsion at this distortion and its effects.

Natural Rights

Changing theoretical views after the American founding dimmed our understanding of rights. They even more completely distorted our understanding of nature.

Arguments following Kant's works at the end of the eighteenth century stopped seeing nature as a measure for human action. The argument became decisive that our central traits change and vary historically and that reason essentially shapes and produces rather than discovers. Even thinkers who supported individual rights increasingly failed to defend them as natural.

It is hard to conserve "natural" rights once thinkers no longer see nature as a standard, or citizens view it at best as a way to discuss animals and the environment, that is, what is not human. Yet, the Declaration of Independence speaks seriously of "the laws of nature and of nature's God," and the thinker whom Thomas Jefferson chiefly had in mind, John Locke, spoke confidently of natural rights.

What does it mean to call our rights "natural" or to say that the laws of nature and Nature's God justify our independence? "Nature" is not a throwaway term. In fact, to ignore the natural basis of rights is to make our preference for them arbitrary, or a mere expression of American habit and tradition. Our rights are "self-evident" truths; that is, they are self-evident to reason. They are visible in principle to all men, not only to some men in some situations. To notice them does not require that one be ensconced in the class, religious, or familial order prized by later conservatives. They are not merely the rights of Americans, Englishmen, the rich, the poor, or any other such group. They belong to all.

Rights are natural because they are evident to reason, belong to each man, and are inalienable. What is natural is, first, what is inevitable and spontaneous rather than arbitrary and artificially concocted. We sometimes ask people to be "natural," by which we mean to be real, not phony, artificial, or made-up. In the last analysis, what is most spontaneous, or least arbitrary, is what is inevitable and unavoidable. The natural is inherent and inescapable in every attempt to ignore or choose against it and in the powers we use to make this choice.

What is natural is also what is general or universal about something, a dog or cat's nature, as we say, or even a person's natural impatience or calm. When what is universal and spontaneous also organizes, directs, and sets in motion something's other qualities, it is fundamental to it. This is why the natural is often the essential or fundamental. The authoritative use of our natural freedom is essentially connected to each of our other actions and pursuits.

The fact that reason recognizes natural truths suggests that what is most natural is what is present most universally, because reason as such sees what is unlimited by the merely bodily, material, local, or transient. For humans, indeed, our ever-present natural ability is reason itself and choice according to it. What is universal about or in something need not cover it identically, however, at least not obviously. Each of us reasons or speaks but not equally well. Sunsets and pictures of sunsets are similar, not identical. All roses are roses but only some bloom with spectacular beauty.

The full range and power of what is universal, spontaneous, and essential is difficult to grasp completely. In the case of natural rights, however, the question is not especially complex, because their substance is the inalienable power everyone has to reflect and choose, to make up his own mind, and to pursue actions under his own direction. Natural rights exist in each of us fully, not only in some average way. Moreover, their immediacy and extent means that everyone can see them not only in principle but in fact, once his vision is freed from theocratic and class occlusions.

Can Nature Guide?

Nature is not only inevitable (spontaneous) and universal, it also guides. This guidance is not obvious, because we flee earthquakes and storms, or try to overcome them. The harshness and destruction of much in the physical world is one reason people wonder how nature can set standards. "According to nature you want to *live*?" Nietzsche asks incredulously:

Imagine a being like nature, wasteful beyond measure, indifferent beyond measure, without purposes and consideration, without mercy and justice, fertile and desolate and uncertain at the same time; imagine indifference itself as a power—how could you live according to this indifference?[5]

One way nature guides is precisely through forces and powers that are present even when we try to manage them. Nature also guides more affirmatively, however, because our human abilities have a complete or satisfactory use and structure, and a natural pleasure, attraction, and beauty connected to them. We do not invent this satisfaction or attraction. Nature supplies forms and ends as well as motions and materials. Natural use and structure set the direction for human improvement, moreover, as proper vision sets the direction for lenses, and even for vision stronger than 20/20.[6] Indeed, nature distinguishes in the sense that, as we said, all men reason, but some better than others.

The true issue is not that natural guidance is simply missing, but that it is disputable and complex. We are what we are only by being free to choose. We therefore can be what we are only by activating and energizing ourselves, and we can do this poorly or have capacities that fall short to begin with. Moreover, the complexity of choice, reason, and their objects is such that the variety of our goals and practices makes easy statements about what and how to choose difficult to give. Reason differentiates us fundamentally, but does not simply constitute us. We are also composed from our desires, loves, spiritedness, and pride and are oriented to the property, wealth, pleasure, beauty, honors, friendships, and knowledge that help to satisfy these passions. The combinations among these goods and the political and social conditions that form and fit them, the competition among us when these goods are scarce, and the differences among us make natural direction obscure. This obscurity exists even if we are oriented toward a measured grasp of these goods, let alone when we are dominated by error and illusion.

This variety notwithstanding, we can still sketch with some precision the goods that most complete our natural powers and reasoned enjoyment of them. Aristotle's discussions in his *Ethics* and *Politics* and Plato's in his *Republic* clarify much of what we can say about natural excellence.

This controversy about guidance, however, concerns the best use of our powers, not the presence of natural rights. One of the great attractions of basing public or political choice on natural rights is precisely their universality, which makes them a visible and stable ground for potential agreement and consent. The evidence for natural free choice is more accessible than is the evidence for the excellent use of this choice.[7] Natural rights are largely open about ends. Any desires (such as bodily desires) that we can fill by exercising equal natural rights (within the political and economic order that equal freedom implies) are acceptable, and in this way natural, not arbitrary.

This general orientation limits the practical effects of the disputes about the proper way of life that are occasioned by the uncertainty and scarcity I just mentioned. The orientation of equal rights toward goods that satisfy desires is compatible with the attempt to acquire and expand resources, moreover, because such growth helps satisfy equally justifiable needs and wants.[8] Distribution of goods according to status and class would be unfairly unequal, while completely equal access to limited or shrinking resources would be dangerous and ineffective. The authority of the natural individual, moreover, correlates well with individual property, because making something my own is the external expression, stamp, or embodiment of authoritative individual choice. Securing individual property therefore is a central task of governments based on individual rights, not a mere accident of British or American history or an imposition by the wealthy.[9]

One might worry that an orientation to property and to equality of desires restricts the excellence of, say, art, religion, thought, and character. Whether this is so is one of the subjects of my later chapters. In any event, as I have said, the presence of natural rights, the presence of the natural authority to choose for myself, is more evident than is guidance about how to use these rights well.[10]

Government and the Natural Individual

Natural rights belong to individuals. One might therefore think that they result in rampant selfishness or boasting, the unending demands of one's own satisfactions, the continual assertion of one's own dignity, the constant demand for rule and respect. This turns out not to be so, for natural rights channel and organize individual pride by recognizing and institutionalizing its rational basis in equality. They therefore provide a ground for generalizing and thus taming or humanizing what might otherwise be the fierce, unfounded,

assertion of one's own dignity or the merely selfish materialism that the individual locus of our natural rights suggests.

Natural rights that we properly institutionalize control
the harmful effects of selfishness and pride in several ways.
We can see this by developing a somewhat beautified or,
as we now say, "idealized" picture. They lead to limited
government, that is, government limited in its purpose,
because government's goal is to secure rights, not institute
an opinion about natural happiness or excellence. Limited
government is not government devoted to heroes and is
therefore not the sole locus of outsized ambition. They lead
to a growing, competitive, economy because wealth is a
largely neutral means to various satisfactions, and because
the individual talents equality frees are primarily directed
to economic action. They lead to vigorous and open inven-
tion for the same reason. The normal result is plenty and
the unleashing of the practical mind, not petty materialism. They lead to growth in education because self-mastery
and self-government demand this. They lead to religious
toleration because the public rule of just one religion distorts the force of equal rights, and the public dominance
of religion generally counters the effectiveness of natural
motives reasonably understood. For these and other reasons,
moreover, countries based on natural rights limit the effect
of extra-political inequality—individual rights do not rest
easily with education restricted to class superiors, or religion grounded in humble obedience to clerics and priests.
Indeed, natural rights are the only true ground of equality,
for they are held equally and permanently by all individuals,
not dispensed "equally" to some by others. They therefore (at

least partially) ground and orient our passion for justice and our wish to institute it. Reason recognizes no rank among individuals at the level of the possibility or necessity of our own self-direction. Equal rights demand the equality of independence, not the equality of misery, subservience, failure, or envy.

The picture, of course, is never as pure as I have just painted it. Countries based on natural rights cannot be simply just. Our way of life supports the character we need to protect our rights but does not guarantee it. The social and institutional conditions we need to use our rights well do not grow automatically. The voluntary, individual, material orientation that liberal democracy promotes even in some respects harms them. The governments that help to secure rights are imperfect, always doing either too much or too little. It is part of conservatism to understand that to conserve individual rights is always to secure them in an imperfect situation here and now. But some situations are less imperfect than others, and we can improve most.

Contemporary Liberalism

When thinkers no longer take nature seriously as the ground of rights, the preference for rights begins to seem arbitrary. This rootless position cannot be sustained. One therefore seeks other ways to understand rights' justice and choice-worthiness; the two centuries since the American founding are filled with such efforts. The major effort since the Second World War to rescue liberalism without natural rights is associated with John Rawls and his students. It attempts to work backwards from what one wishes to protect morally and politically in order to find acceptable grounds from which to derive the desired outcomes. One then makes necessary adjustments as one switches back and forth between the outcomes one desires and the principles one stipulates provisionally. This effort cannot satisfactorily underpin politics and morality, however, if it merely looks to one's own preferences. So, one seeks to ground what "we" wish.

Many acute analyses emerge from this method. The problem of the injustice of some inequalities in wealth is especially usefully highlighted. Nonetheless, the philosophical status of the procedure proves ambiguous because its starting point is arbitrary. It is not natural, as John Locke and our founders have in mind, for it does not dwell on natural authority or on the "state of nature," the constantly threatening and penurious conditions that obtain when we each assert individual authority unlimited by government. Nor does this procedure take root in an unavoidable link between reason and freedom, as argued by thinkers such as Kant or Hegel. The connection between recognizing one's inalienable natural authority and recognizing one's responsibilities, talents, and ends is therefore obscured. Indeed, the procedure proves finally to be for and about an impossible being.

To confront the difficulty of philosophical ambiguity (among other reasons) one sometimes argues that the grounds one seeks were never meant to be philosophical. Rather, they are political or public grounds. But these turn out to be general opinions floating in a netherworld between constitutions and the theoretical analysis and description that might justify them. Such "grounds" make it easy to change one's assertions about freedom, equality, talents, groups, and individuals at will because these assertions need not fit coherently. They are therefore intellectually unsatisfactory.

The other, related, difficulty with such defenses of liberalism is the status of the "we" whose views need grounding. One finds general talk about people who require rules for cooperation but have no specific ends that form their venture. They therefore have no reasons to exclude anyone from it. Root equality of participation and contribution is taken for granted, not justified; an author can therefore adjust and readjust the substance of cooperative equality and freedom until he achieves the results he seeks. "We" in practice in such discussions turns out to be people roughly such as ourselves, but with currently fashionable left-liberal views, especially as they fester among today's constitutional law professors. The unsurprising result is that the theories justify or demand various types of substantive equality that whittle away at individual freedom.

This bias and arbitrariness result in contemporary liberal defenses of liberal democracy that cover up the true links among natural rights, economic growth, limited government, free and vigorous political speech, and the priority of individual action to social imposition. Not everything in these theories is valueless but their impetus is misguided.

The Appeal of Liberty

The dominance of natural rights results in regimes that help to provide plenty. It therefore ameliorates the economic problem of scarce resources. It also helps to provide a safe outlet for political energy because it encourages entrepreneurial private action and political competition. It thus overcomes better than other authorities the political problem of scarce power or rule that leads to violent struggle. And it does so without destroying enterprising political spirit.

The power of liberty's appeal lies not merely in these effects, which vary in strength and extent, but also in its clarity, universality, and desirability. Anyone can see quickly that his own ability to prefer and to choose is unshakeable and inevitable. This clear, indubitable, universal presence and desirability differentiates liberty from other grounds that one may consider fundamental, such as religious grounds that we do not share generally or are matters of faith. One's own self-examination shows the existence of one's freedom of preference and choice. For this reason, an appeal to freedom always strikes a chord, because it is an appeal to something one sees in oneself.

The heart of modern conservatism is the individual stance favored by individual rights. American liberalism, which once shared this stance, has exchanged it step by sometimes unwitting step for ethnic, gender, and class preference, government that equalizes and often punishes arbitrarily rather than regulates effectively, and thoughtless opinions that talk of natural rights and self-evident truths as dispensable cultural anachronisms. The standpoint of individual rights, by contrast, is the best ground on which to liberate most of us from suffocation by groups, classes, and ethnicities, or by ascriptive and irrational authority generally. It is the heart of self-government and of protection from control by others who claim to know one better than one knows oneself.

The conservative appeal to liberty is effective above all because it speaks to something truly desired and simple to recognize. Individual liberty actually is the heart of our founding; it is not a merely asserted and concocted ground. Each can see that it is natural and naturally desirable for himself, not a passing preference. Its appeal is not only effective, moreover, it deserves to be effective, individually and politically. For, liberty contains an unmistakable core of self-direction and self-control even if politicians often evoke it with nothing rigorous in mind. Actual independence requires character and effort, even when some confuse "liberty" with complete abandon for which someone else should foot the bill. It also speaks to justice, because natural rights are genuinely held equally and failure to acknowledge this provokes justified indignation.[11] Individual liberty is the core of what American conservatism should properly seek to conserve.

To understand and act on this view of liberty is important for the country's common good. It is not only beneficial for the members of a movement or party. Such an appeal, however, is today especially vital to the health of Republicans, because arguments that appeal chiefly to group identities favor Democrats. Of course, we have good reasons to want two strong parties even if one is largely a satellite of the other, and even if the primary party's ideas are not very good. It is useful if a relatively safe and sane group is available to pick up the pieces when the primary party disgusts the electorate through scandal, mismanagement, and policy overreach.

Best would be two organized representatives of essentially the same conservative standards. A party manager, however, must concern himself with recruiting candidates and funds, and with pursuing tactical advantage. These measures are easier for parties that stand for something, but they differ from principled action itself. To wish to conserve liberty is not to be simply partisan, even if events require what seems to be partisanship.

CHAPTER TWO

Conserving Virtue

Conservatism of the sort I am defending faces typical objections. We cannot support it convincingly while ignoring them. I will argue that individual freedom provides the best ground on which to counteract these objections appropriately. But we are unable to meet them altogether. What is true in the objections should bring forward the modesty that ought to belong to all conservatism, even when we are conserving our new and radical principles.

I will begin with one major objection to individual liberty, namely, that it is inherently selfish—that it lacks compassion, generosity, attention to others, and altruism. I will then discuss the related but broader objection that the love of individual gain in free regimes diminishes human character by failing to support moral virtue. I will first report some facts about philanthropy in order to set a reasonable base for discussing character. I will then explore the distinctive virtues that our founding liberalism supports, and say a word about traditional virtues. In general, conservative liberalism advances much individual excellence of soul, but it also partially counters the conditions for its flourishing.

Selfishness

A typical argument against conservative liberalism is that it encourages selfishness. We become purely self-interested acquirers of material goods. Any devotion to friends, family, church, and country is merely a fading echo of earlier epochs. It will soon be dissolved in the corrosive bath of selfishness. We already see this decline in the diminishing attention to family and the decreasing number of middle and upper middle class children.

The contemporary charge of selfishness is not ordinarily made in the name of virtue, whose celebration also stems from an older point of view. Rather, it usually belongs to concern about the decline of altruism and community. This worry is often expressed by today's liberal intellectuals, and sometimes comes from academic quarters whose residents' devotion to something other than themselves is well hidden.

Indeed, such criticism belongs today to the usual argument for expanding the state, not redirecting it to help secure the conditions for individual excellence. "Justice," or "social justice," or equal justice is the quality whose absence is most often decried. Its absence is decried not because it impoverishes the soul, but as a fact of maldistribution, of inequality. It is the state, not each of us privately, that must step in to redistribute resources, provide goods such as health, and improve results for favored groups.

The facts that these practices distort economic action and reduce economic growth slow the pace of government imposition, but not for long and rarely permanently. The imposition still seems correct, just, and right to today's liberals, held back by the needs of production, not by a judgment of their illiberalism.

Philanthropy

The charge of selfish unconcern seems reasonable at first glance, because pursuing individual rights is not obviously connected to helping others. It differs from immediate self-understanding in terms of a group, and it is this (restricted) empathy that seems to be the chief source of concern for others. Yet, arguments from well before Adam Smith himself have made evident the odd truth that under the right circumstances helping oneself helps others. This unintended aid may be important, one might counter, but it lacks the moral worth that comes from intended selflessness. Yet, the claim that few intentionally help others when we are primarily executing our own rights is in truth belied by the facts of American voluntarism and philanthropy, and by general agreement with at least some of our government's mandate of substantial transfers of wealth. Americans gave $307 billion in the economically difficult year of 2008, down from the previous year, but up from 2003's $240.7. Arbitrarily cut this number in half on the assumption that much of it goes to institutions (say churches and private schools) that help one and one's own much more directly than they help others and the number is still very large. Sixty three million Americans report volunteering 8.1 billion hours in 2009. At $20.85 per hour we arrive at a value of $169 billion. Cut this too in half—cut it by two-thirds—on the assumption that people are exaggerating, that the Independent Sector, which calculates this amount, has arbitrarily inflated an already too high number, and that not many would pay for much of the time that is volunteered.[1] We would nonetheless have $55–85 billion for the value of volunteering. A total that summed our cautious numbers for philanthropy and volunteerism would still give us over $200 billion.

One might then claim that these practices of philanthropy and volunteering derive from today's liberals. For, they are the ones concerned with the justice of equality simply, not merely equality of rights. They therefore spearhead attempts to transfer wealth from rich to poor. Or, one might suggest that our philanthropy stems from group loyalty, memory of traditional duties, or echoes of traditional *noblesse oblige* (i.e., that it stems from what traditional conservatism celebrates). It is traditional conservatism or contemporary liberalism, but not the securing of individual rights that causes the philanthropy we admire. We might then reply that it is our breadth of free choice that allows us philanthropic choices as well as selfish ones. But one could then claim that the motives and loyalties that encourage these philanthropic choices are based on the views and lives we have just mentioned. Were individual liberty to be triumphant, the selflessness for which it praises itself by looking at philanthropic largesse would piece by piece disappear. Its triumph would destroy the grounds for the activities it admires.

These factors of traditional conservatism and egalitarian liberalism are significant. Nevertheless, I will argue that individual liberty can and does support voluntarism, philanthropy, and public concern from its own ethical resources. It is not simply or primarily selfish. Indeed, we can successfully exercise equally held individual rights only if we also develop certain virtues of character. Otherwise, we will be overwhelmed by competition, and by the difficulty of succeeding when so little is determined in advance. This virtue, in turn, together with the economic plenty advanced by liberty, serves others as well as oneself.

Virtue

Why is virtue important? Character is composed from dispositions or habits that guide action. Good habits are virtuous ones; they are directed by practical reason. In Aristotle's classic understanding, virtue concerns particular goods and passions—courage not cowardice when faced with fear, moderation not license when faced with pleasure, liberality not stinginess when giving gifts.

Some virtues are broader than these in their object, and not restricted to a primary field. Industry is virtue and laziness vice in relation to many goods. Indeed, the characteristic virtues in liberal society—those dispositions we see or consider to be virtues today but did not praise earlier—have this breadth. They are connected to the wide range of equally satisfactory objects of desire that we allow to be pursued in liberal life.

The importance of virtue is not primarily that good communities require it. Cowards and criminals are of course to be despised, but virtue's deeper significance is that happiness, merit, and human excellence are largely composed of virtues of the soul. One goal of political life is to help secure conditions for individual happiness, and virtue is a central element of this happiness. It elevates the powers of the soul— our passions, our loves, our spiritedness—coordinates them with our reason, and makes possible the regular exercise of intelligent choice. Virtue is primarily an end for us, not only a means, say, to wealth or military security.

Virtue and Rights

The view that economic individualism and virtue are disjunctive became so extreme that for a time writers ignored the connection between virtue and liberty altogether, or mocked whatever virtues they noticed. Some, D.H. Lawrence, Stendhal, and Baudelaire, for example, made fun of Benjamin Franklin and his autobiographical list. But this required closing themselves to Franklin's irony, or never reading him in the first place.[2] Indeed, even if, say, Horatio Alger's heroes are not Achilles, they are not amoral. One can see that his and Franklin's bourgeois virtues are still virtues.

The intellectual fact that leads to overlooking or denigrating liberal virtues is that the philosophical origin of natural rights in Hobbes and Locke seemed not to leave room for excellence of character. As part of the effort to institute natural individualism, Aristotle's thought and Christian authority were attacked directly and indirectly. Acquisition and accumulation became the goal. Satisfaction was pleasure, the occasional short-term filling of desire. The worth of pleasure was separated from ranking the desires it satisfied; pleasures were all commensurable. Property and satisfaction were alone what mattered. Virtue understood as what guides the use of goods, and virtues as differentiated by the goods they used well—bodily pleasure, wealth, beauty, honor—lost their cogency or were no longer understood. Even when one saw that we need honesty, trust, and industry economically, they appeared more as means to wealth than as choiceworthy in themselves. And even if voluntary contracts require honesty, they especially require police: the believable threat trumps the remote good habit. Self-sacrifice and fighting in wars were for oneself at best necessities, not noble actions. Virtue as a goal, as the term for the excellences that wealth and freedom served, faded from view. It became a name for a tradesman's probity or a woman's chastity, the quality that allows others to believe that you are unlikely or afraid to cheat.

From this standpoint, those who doubt the link between virtue and the bourgeois life that natural rights promote are more reasonable than those who deny the discrepancy between them. "Virtues" that are mere means to ends—virtues such as ordinary honesty and hard work—do not attract one's full effort, use one's full powers, or stand out with special beauty or allure. They belong to what is finally the pointless exercise of freedom. An industrious hamster is still a hamster.

Virtue Resurgent

During the past twenty-five or so years scholars have tried to correct this picture of liberal vice or indifference, and liberal virtues are much discussed.[3] Analyses waver between reasserting the existence of the typical bourgeois virtues and trying to show that liberal life also permits or requires more complete and choiceworthy characteristics. This attempt allows one to notice, or is guided by noticing, the powerful thinkers from Smith to Hegel who did not teach a necessary connection between individual rights and moral vulgarity. It enables one to take a fresh look at Hobbes, Locke, and the American founders.[4] It permits one to recognize and seek the grounds for the apparently inexplicable existence in liberal democracies of philanthropy, willingness to serve in armies, and widespread fairness and trust.

This fresh look recovers, discovers, and elevates the place of virtues in free regimes. But good reasons still exist not to confuse virtue in liberal democracy with virtue simply, or in all respects. For, virtues that are oriented to exercising equal individual rights are constrained by equality. They are also limited by the fact that activities and goods in liberal democracies first strike us as things we are equally free to want, equally free to purchase, and equally free to attempt. There is no immediate directing of our desires or ranking of goods. Critics of bourgeois life often speak of its flatness: the equating and equal accessibility of goods is one thing they have in mind.

Connected to this flatness is that majority tastes become favored: novelty; easy, untrained, enjoyment; trivia; celebrity without achievement. Given our equality, volume and size willy-nilly become criteria of attention and investment. Arts tend to be equated, so all beauty is diminished. Pleasant but fleeting leisure must be available to everyone, so we waste much on silliness. The virtue classically connected to beauty, magnificence, is therefore hardly recognizable. Moderation cannot survive the onslaught of bizarre but legal pleasures. Courage in battle is limited to a few; for others it exists if at all only on a smaller field. Wit is vulgarized. Friendship is largely commercial, and friendliness is empty and surface. Self-government—the field for the great-souled pursuit of distinction or honor—is dwarfed by a combination of bureaucracy, legalism, patronage, and dynasty. Acting justly becomes merely minimum obedience in a world of increasingly peculiar laws. Practical judgment loses its way in a forest of expertise. "Wisdom" becomes narrowed to specialized knowledge. Intelligence favors quantitative tests, natural sciences, law schools, and academic rigidity. In general, then, the goods with which the virtues deal are leveled, and the opportunities to enjoy them are diminished. The Aristotelian excellences that weigh and coordinate these goods are consequently also debased, ignored, or fade away altogether.

These strictures against regimes based on natural rights are telling but excessive. The criticisms are distorted because they are measured against pictures, not facts. The classic virtues still remain recognizable. Many in liberal democracies are courageous, moderate, and generous. Vulgarity has not altogether replaced beauty. The cacophony of artistic mediocrity still leaves a place for excellence. Indifference to beauty has not eliminated magnificent private action for public benefit: consider, say, philanthropy in the arts. We have statesmen of some rank, moreover, and even in the past century more than one near the highest rank. Our politics permit and demand much self-government, however restricted. The fact that almost all (legal) actions first come to light as equally choiceworthy, or that it is acceptable for the talented to spend their lives defending people who produce foolish movies or make soft drinks has not eliminated a separate, nuanced, understanding of proper and worthwhile behavior. What seems to be the overwhelming effect of liberal equality in goals and choices does not in fact efface a natural view of the hierarchy of goods. The political and social conditions consequent to natural rights do not altogether push aside the conditions we need for excellence. The charge that to conserve liberalism is to conserve mediocrity and to flatten virtue is overdrawn.

Liberal Virtues

It is not merely that these strictures are overblown. There are also distinctively liberal virtues that replace some of what is lost. We should see that individual rights and regimes based on them give rise to distinctive virtues of their own. None of these virtues deals with a distinctive good. Each is debased if we fail to see its ground in individuals, not groups. Nonetheless, some are genuine excellences that require judgment, although none, save responsibility, governs, forms, or controls truly forceful passion.

Four virtues that regimes of liberty advance and that conservatism should conserve are industriousness, toleration,
considerateness (niceness), and responsibility. They are virtues because they are dispositions of soul. They are habits
of choosing and of acting once judgment is made, not mere
calculations that are largely episodic. In each case the virtue
advances one's ability to execute one's rights while also limiting mere selfishness or the dominance of pride. One needs
these virtues for success but (or because) they also fit with
helping to satisfy others' needs.

Hard Work

I begin with industriousness or hard work, for it is a virtue
too equal and general, too tied to necessity, and too distinct
from using leisure well to be seen as virtue classically. It is
a trait we have in mind when we talk of "bourgeois" virtues. To be industrious is to be diligent and to persevere
doggedly in one's tasks, whatever they are. One could be
equally industrious about painting something beautiful and
painting the side of a barn. As a virtue, it does not attend
to differences among goods. Even thieves can be industrious. To be industrious is not uplifting: it does not require a
skyward glance. It is to move from one item to another, to
do one thing after another, until what is for the moment the
last item is finished. The barn is painted until someone calls
for a second coat. Industry does not require one to grasp the
full purpose of one's action, the big picture, as we say.

One is especially industrious about accumulating the
wealth or store of goods that enables one to enjoy satisfactions, whatever they turn out to be. Without this virtue, or

outstanding luck, one will fail in a liberal world where each exercises his own freedom and calls on others to do so too. But industriousness alone does not make one happy. It is not even a central component of happiness. It is a means to an end, not a shining excellence. But it is preferable to sloth and inattention, and it is a virtue of character especially promoted and preserved by the free economies that are coordinate with liberty.

Tolerance

A second liberal virtue one does not see among the ancients— nor among the Christians—is tolerance. To be tolerant is to allow people to do things their own way, especially if one disapproves of that way. In particular, tolerance is the disposition grudgingly to permit others to practice their religion. The others one tolerates are individuals, not groups as such, for we practice tolerance because we see religion as primarily private and voluntary. Were it not, a change in government could be too dangerous for believers to accept. To tolerate does not mean to help or advance—one merely "tolerates." A man who acts tolerantly will not help others to preserve their faith by permitting illegal practices or by enforcing religious mandates. Nor will he tolerate the intolerant, unless this poses no threat.

Toleration comes into being as a virtue once modern thinkers attempt to reduce religion's public place. Toleration does not require prayer and legally binding punishment of disbelievers. On the contrary, it tends to make faith a matter of choice. In this sense toleration is not strictly neutral. For, to sequester piety and ritual in the realm of private choice is to reduce religion's public place and to weaken or transform religions that require legal enforcement and public support. As a public virtue toleration replaces piety, or humble obedience to a particular god or gods, and the orthodoxy of correct practices and opinions.

It is a mark of the weakening of liberal individualism that some now think that toleration requires us to support actively those we merely tolerate. It is also a mark of its weakening that the object of tolerance has spread from religion to "lifestyles," groups, and preferences generally. It is a further mark of its weakening that people—intellectuals especially—are so uncertain about how much one should tolerate the illiberal. They have forgotten that a regime of liberty is meant to restrict the scope of illiberal practices by making them private and voluntary, that, in the long run it means to dissolve the attraction of illiberalism and to advance the attraction of liberty, and that when we tolerate illiberal practices, we do so not on principle but from strength. Tolerance has become distorted by relativism and by the niceness, decency, considerateness, or even-handedness that also belong to liberalism. Indeed, tolerance itself tends blandly to equalize religious heights and strong secular differences even when one sees it as self-withholding from punishing what one disapproves. To conserve this virtue would also be to return from its growing flaccidity to the seriousness and inner strength suggested by "mere" tolerance and "grudging" approval.

Considerateness

A third distinctively liberal virtue is to be considerate, or, in its current weaker and flabbier version, to be "nice." To be considerate is to leave room for others while pursuing one's own interests. It is more to withhold—not to be inconsiderate or mean—than it is to be terribly helpful. To be considerate is to be disposed to be neither selfishly inconsiderate nor to ask too much. Especially when being considerate fades into being nice, it is also to be flexible rather than to apply rules and regulations inflexibly or to make what others believe are narrow-minded and excessive demands. It is also to be generally pleasant rather than prickly, distant, or difficult, to show an easy if largely surface familiarity. Someone who is nice pleasantly considers other people's interests and feelings and does not always require that his own interests and feelings, or the rules that he administers, take precedence. Being nice in this way is an American characteristic that Europeans used to point out, to praise, blame, or mock.

As with industriousness, no special content or excellence exists in the interests or goods about which one is flexible and considerate. Both being nice and being industrious are dispositions for dealing with things and others that do not take their lead from the substance of action.

The call to be considerate is especially heard today politically, when one asks partisans to listen to each other, or to be "civil." The need for the request shows the presence of its opposite; everyone notices growing incivility in political debates and campaigns and among media-partisans. The sensible wish is to recognize others' equal right to speak and not to interrupt rudely, and to refrain from calling opponents names that if taken seriously would cast them outside the pale of respectable liberal democracy. The call, however, sometimes mistakes civility for nicely refraining from asserting one's own opinions, or for limiting partisanship.

More, the call sometimes confuses civility with agreement, or wishes to restrict debate unduly: the bedrock of the agreement one craves turns out to be some version of one's own liberal views, not the law, constitution, and good character.[5] In this sense, the demand for civility fits with branches of contemporary liberalism that believe it crucial to set in advance what counts as deliberative equality. One result is to substitute current professorial views of good evidence and acceptable process for people's actual assertion of rights, interests, and arguments grounded in the Constitution. A second effect is to substitute substantive political equality for the legitimacy of actual majority rule whether asserted or not. The effect is also to downplay substantive arguments we make to defend liberal democracy against other regimes, arguments that bring out the connections among liberty, self-interest, and plenty. The model is legalistic rather than political; it both restricts and makes too rigid what counts as a good argument. It also harmfully usurps the concept of "deliberation," understood previously as the general name for the practical reasoning that is coordinate with ethical virtue.[6]

All three virtues that we are discussing belong to a way of life that is grounded on equally held individual rights. This way of life makes others' interests in principle equal to my own. My freedom and what I do with it come first, because of the inescapable separateness for me of my own reasoned choice and self-direction, and, therefore, of my own pride and needs. But one's freedom is equal to others', so there is no dominant or inherent rank. These three modern virtues deal with others in a way that either helps to provide for them, as industriousness does, or preserves an arena for their equal actions as do considerateness and tolerance. There is nothing especially uplifting about them, but they are real and they help us see that conservative individualism is not mere self-interest or vanity.[7]

Responsibility

A fourth characteristically modern virtue is responsibility, which first begins to be discussed around the time of the American founding. We prize the self-reliance associated with it. Responsibility names the chief disposition one needs to secure and advance one's own freedom, and to achieve success in filling one's desires. It also helps to explain the individual proclivity to act effectively in the public interest, beyond the forbearance that tolerance and niceness suggest. There are reasons why American presidents praise it even while ignoring or corrupting it.

Although we usually think of responsibility as accountability, and consider it in a context of guilt, punishment, and blame, to be responsible is also, and primarily, to be effective, to succeed, to accomplish, to get the job done. Responsibility is the disposition to do what it takes to succeed, and to be accountable for success—accountable to the one for whom one works, but, primarily, accountable to oneself. Mere accountability is not enough to explain responsibility because it focuses on blame rather than achievement, on effort rather than success, and on following proper procedure in order to show that one is guilt-free, even if unsuccessful or incompetent. Responsibility as accountability for success may sometimes need to accept failed effort, of course, because one fully controls nothing. Unlike those concerned with mere accountability, however, responsible men are not content to avoid blame by displaying effort even if fruitless. Indeed, a responsible man wants to put as much under his control as he can, because his disposition is to succeed, not to avoid blame. And, he is much more likely to despise useless or harmful procedure than to hide behind it.

Responsibility is an important virtue in liberal democracies because one must be responsible in order to execute one's freedom and to place it out into the world. The unavoidable fact of one's own choice and reflection does not bring with it the ability to choose well continually, to amass property, or even, in some cases, to survive. When all occupations are open to so many and duties of class and locality so diminished, when tradition fades and one is thrown back upon oneself, one must gather in oneself the training and capacities to be successful and to continue to be successful. Opportunities expand in regimes of liberty, including the opportunity to fail.

Responsibility and Public Spirit

Responsibility is the disposition to be effective, now and in the future. It therefore involves developing the diligence, attention, effort, and skills one needs to be self-reliant and free. Its attention to success, and to the conditions for one's success, moreover, is able and in some cases impelled to take on a breadth that supports or initiates action for others' good. Because the desires and aspirations that help to define one's self are, for anyone in liberal democracy, so open, one is able to grasp one's self and one's responsibilities, the arenas where one effectuates one's liberties, expansively. One can place oneself in or be responsible for more and more. One can shape more and more. One can try to manage, or make one's presence felt in, or bring about, more and more. Some, indeed, see that the conditions for their own success expand beyond themselves narrowly. They understand that perpetuating the conditions and possibilities of their own free effectiveness requires that some place themselves in wider domains, and come to see themselves as the ones responsible for the perpetuation. So, from responsibility for oneself and one's family one becomes responsible for one's business enterprise, for schools and local governments, for hospitals and museums, for the country as a whole. None of this wider responsibility departs simply from serving one's own interest while one is serving a broader interest, but one is indeed also serving broader interests. The responsible men and women who run for office, direct school boards, and support charities are not altruists. They help themselves as they help others. Responsibility is neither self-denial nor disguised selfishness.

Those who attend to public tasks choose and assert expansive freedom and a broad view of what their future effectiveness requires, in a competition that is open to all. Responsibility thus differentiates people who are nonetheless still equal in their rights, and differentiates them apart from their different desires. Not all are equally responsible or place themselves in greater and greater enterprises. The fullest responsibilities belong to statesmen, but responsibility in all cases disposes one to some degree of self-government. No one need take on public tasks in liberal democracies, because they are open to all and prescribed for none. Yet, it is not surprising that many do, because some come to place their freedom and responsibility in these wider spheres. For, if we do not act for ourselves, who will act for us?

Such broad responsibility could even become a disposition hard to distinguish in some from ancient greatness of soul, were it not for equal rights under law, competition among those in principle equal, and control dispersed among so many enterprises. Responsibility is compelling enough in what it requires that it may attractively shape one's whole soul and actions, as other modern virtues and many ancient virtues do not. If one were nothing but responsible one would still be considerable. Yet, it is not virtue's peak simply. For, it is always twinned with and therefore directed by the equal freedom that it makes effective and is not the full happiness that simply noble action or playfully considering the beautiful can be.

Modern Virtue

The typically modern virtues help explain why modern individualism does not merely become vulgar self-interest, endless accumulation, self-isolation, or domineering pride. These virtues shape and ennoble character, for they are dispositions, not passing calculations. Conserving liberty also means conserving free regimes' characteristic human excellences, whatever their limits.

We must not ignore the importance of classic virtues, for the range of modern choice enables us to select them too.

They remain naturally attractive. But the conditions under which classic virtue flourishes and is praised fade in liberal democracies, and in some cases contradict it. This seems especially true of magnanimity and magnificence. These are difficult to conserve when honor and politics are degraded and bureaucratized, and when we mistake the vulgar for the beautiful. Were there nothing in liberal democracy's own resources to support virtue the difficulty would be greater. Indeed, this difficulty of preservation is true of the typically liberal virtues too, which we weaken and misinterpret in the directions I sketched. To conserve even liberal virtues is a hard task.

Justice

Much criticism of conservatism concerns inequality. Opportunity seems unfairly distributed, and success much easier for some to attain than for others. Gaps in income are thought to be too great. Poverty remains too high.[8] The heart of these criticisms concerns justice, for difference in income and status is justified if at all by a standard, and the leading standard in liberal democracy is equality.

I will begin my discussion of justice by developing these criticisms. My purpose is to suggest again the significance of equal rights as the basis for equal treatment. I will then discuss justice more broadly in two respects, as following proper authority, and as giving equal to equals and unequal to unequals. I will attempt to show how regimes of liberty are just in these senses, but also will indicate limits to their justice.

Equality in rights leads to different outcomes because people's circumstances, talents, skills, and luck differ. To equalize these outcomes one would need to control the free use of rights, or to adjust results. One could press equalizing so far that freedom would be radically restricted. But radically restricting the rights whose securing is the purpose of the equalizing is self-defeating.[9] Or, one might suggest that we depend on government, family, and social institutions so much that everything we are belongs to a whole: individuality of rights is a false standpoint. No responsibility exists without family and no enterprise without police. All one "owns" is in principle at the beck and call of whatever group one needs to be and become what one is.[10] It may equalize to the degree it thinks necessary.

One sees versions of this communal standpoint both in traditional conservatism (although there it fits with inequalities and restrictions on accumulating property and entering occupations) and in some contemporary liberalism (including its communitarian variety) which claims one is primarily dependent or situated, not individual. These views deny the salience or even the existence of one's possession of the talents that lead to unequal results—their true bearer is the community, not oneself.

In both cases, the truth of one's root natural independence is ignored and the link between my natural authority and my responsibility is overlooked. Society's contribution to my efforts is therefore overstated.[11] My rights are in truth fundamentally mine, and unless I control my talents and rewards I am unlikely to use them energetically and effectively (although this does not mean that I will always use them properly).

Without free possession, free choice is economically and politically empty. This link suggests the error of equalizing wealth for equalizing's sake, and provides a motive for the inventiveness and effort that will benefit others as well as myself.

Given natural rights, the goal of any common provision or equalizing of conditions and opportunities is to aid the authority of the free and responsible individual. This purpose restricts the just scope of common actions to what secures everyone's independence. Liberal democracies properly advance *this* kind of common justice and often advance it successfully, economically and educationally. The central way that liberal regimes are just is by providing the punishments, regulations, and encouragements that allow individual rights to be exercised and enjoyed.

The conservatism I am defending does not favor unjustified privilege. It is based on equal rights, equal liberty, equal access to markets, and positions awarded on demonstrated merit. Equality of opportunity is its watchword. Equality of opportunity, however, is not self-generating. It belongs to domains that were once controlled unfairly and used to take from others and tyrannize over them. One such domain is property. Another is education. Freedom leads to some material inequality but also to growth: most material plenty is not limited inherently. We encourage self-reliance not only to advance liberty and virtue but also to produce growth that makes forced equality unnecessary and inequalities less significant. One purpose of regimes of liberty is to stimulate free effort that results in outsized talents producing for common as well as individual benefit, where common benefit primarily means expansion in property.[12] To make merit useful for all, of course, requires regulations that control barriers to entry and monopolies. The greatest unfairnesses, in any event, are ascriptive, not individual.

Justice and Obedience

To explore these matters more completely it helps to discuss justice more fully. To act justly is, first, to obey the law. This is easy to overlook because we see that law is often unjust. Just law concerns (among other matters) properly initiated commands and obedience to them. One reason I use this formulation is to remind us of the link between law and religion. For, law is not always statute law but, rather, religious law. The Old Testament is the law. The Ten Commandments produce obligations.

A just law means in these cases that it is revealed, that it originates from God. In the secular instances of this sense, "just" law means that whatever law's content it stems from properly constituted or legitimate authorities. This split between origin and substance is especially clear with statute law (where a legitimate law may be a foolish one) because revealed law's divine origin should fit with its substance. The Ten Commandments are meant to be just and good in their content, not only because of their source.

Justice as obedience to duly originated law is connected to righteousness as the way to behave and act properly, apart from results. This is clear in the link between justice and piety, reverence, ritual, and orthodoxy. To act justly is to act in a certain way, to follow the rules, to take the prescribed steps, to observe the mandated forms. In liberal democracy, one respects the equality of one's fellow citizens, and oneself as citizen, by following the country's political forms and honoring their results. A duly elected senator serves even if surpassingly mediocre. From this point of view, liberal democracy replaces divine authority with massed individual authority (i.e., with representation).

One might wonder what good comes from justice understood this way.[13] For, acting rightly, observantly, correctly may not bring good results. One good our new political authoritativeness helps to secure is stability. Indeed, observing our forms is central in protecting our free government, whatever its radical roots. What is more conservative than obeying elections whose outcomes we abhor? Respect for due origin helps in advance to neutralize conflict. Disputing the substance of duly constituted law does not relieve one's obligation to obey it. Nonetheless, an excessive split between what is legally, formally, ritually, or procedurally just and what is good can lead to procedure for procedure's sake, observance for observance's sake, ritual for its own sake. It can promote the punctiliousness that allows the guilty to go unpunished or the useful to go unrewarded.

Justice as following properly initiated procedures and ways apart from immediate outcomes can also protect individual dignity, revere the inviolable, hold separate the deservedly independent, and allow each to be treated properly, not merely employed. In our case, proper form based on each citizen's legal equality is central to protecting equal rights. Moreover, such formal action also helps to provide substantive goods. Economic growth needs security from arbitrary intervention by others into one's affairs. Legal procedure allows predictability, zones of exclusivity, and protection of talent. Law that supports one's inviolability can lead one to elevate oneself or not treat oneself merely as an object of instant satisfaction. Indeed, this is its central effect. For us, justly doing things the right way and honoring the outcome is fundamental to the seriousness of individual responsibility (i.e., fundamental to the seriousness of securing individual rights). Equalizing or adjusting outcomes is always harmful because it weakens this, even if in some instance the harm is outweighed.

As I suggested, the merely legal can advance injustice if ritual or observance traps or denies talent arbitrarily, is too separate from providing and enjoying goods substantively, or permits arbitrary or tyrannical control by some (e.g., extremist Islam). Just authority should observe natural rights. Justice cannot only be due constitution, moreover, or be understood as the "purity" of "righteous" behavior. For, justice also means distribution by merit. To what degree do regimes of liberty conserve justice understood in this broader sense?

Justice and Excellence

The simplest examples of such justice concern unequal talents and unequally good instruments. It is just that the better violin goes to the better player. Otherwise, the better instrument and artist are less beautiful than they could be. Justice as putting resources in the best hands is grounded in the connection between natural talents and natural goods. From what standpoint do we determine natural fit? If all that matters is violins and violinists, the issue is easy and easier still where there is no shortage of fine instruments. But what if the better violin is owned by a wealthy mediocrity? Property modifies distribution based on merit. One thought behind common ownership in the beautiful city of Plato's *Republic* is that ownership of goods must be coordinated with their best use, not with property grounded on other claims. For, these claims are not based on distributive merit, but on different facts—first possession, work, contracts, inheritance, or, generally, attachment to oneself and what one loves. In this sense, individual property expresses equal authoritative freedom, and self-interest. We primarily ground just possession on what results from exercising our energies, efforts, and skills, not simply on who makes best use of some good. The equality is in opportunity and rights, and the inequalities result from work, inheritance, calculation, and luck. We make just distribution concrete in property law, which looks to legitimate ownership connected to one's own actions, not to claims of best use. Equal freedom and its correlative virtues primarily connect distribution to effort, and to what is one's own.

Liberal democracy does partially recognize justice as best distribution, but primarily privately, not publicly. Claims of better use are central in distributing or using what we own or control. Still, no perfect relation is present between excellence and equal rights, and there are obvious discrepancies. Nonetheless, some connection does exist: we need freedom to pursue energetically what is excellent; private aspiration and institutions can support much that is excellent; and, expansion of economic goods reduces scarcity and increases leisure.

Summary

To conserve natural rights is to conserve fundamental equality. To do justice is primarily to observe this equality, legally. The characteristically liberal virtues support justice because considerateness and tolerance make room for others and counter the imperial tendencies of self-interest, while industry and responsibility encourage the self-reliance and likely success of equal selves.

Equality in rights, however, can surely lead to unequal wealth, unequal use of education, and other substantive inequalities because differences exist in talent, energy, virtue, and luck. These inequalities do not dissolve fundamental equality but they weaken its expression because they affect opportunities.

Perhaps the two clearest places where we can justify some assured public provision (and in this sense equalizing) of goods are education and access to property, for without these little true self-direction and freedom exist. Such provision is just if it helps protect rights whose use would otherwise be truncated excessively. We do not want so to control and distort talent because of fears of inequality, however, that we erroneously restrict the growth of goods.

Liberty's spirit is to help others through private effort and responsibility, so that they can come to do important things for themselves. Private action for this purpose is insufficient: we must use everyone's taxes to help fund public education, and to pay for market regulations, police, the military, and goods such as public parks. But private action may more easily provide such goods than we currently believe.

Liberalism and Virtue's Decline

Conservatism needs especially to attend to conserving virtue because liberal democracy tends to diminish it either by misinterpreting its meaning or by restricting the conditions for its exercise. Relativism, converting equal rights into substantive demands, and judging and rewarding in terms of groups and classes distort virtue, just as they distort freedom. This is true both for liberal and classic virtues. When we see tolerance as mild forbearance for all differences rather than as grudging acceptance of different religious practices, we weaken standards and obscure religion's unique importance. When cool considerateness becomes excessive flexibility or failure to assert one's own way, when it is merely being passively nice, effort declines and we reduce our sense of the rank among good things. When because of special privilege, government intervention, and business error we break the link between industry and reward, the virtue of hard work fades. Decline is especially pressing with responsibility, for the more government does for us the less we do for ourselves, and the more remote large, complex bureaucracy becomes the less we take charge politically.

Liberal democracy's goal is not freedom alone. The character that lets us use and direct freedom is central to it, and elevates us. Intrusive government, barriers to entry, and family decline harm virtue as well as liberty. One reason conservatives need to conserve virtue is that the policies of today's liberals, and even some of their own actions, often diminish it.

CHAPTER THREE

Conserving Excellence

The heart of contemporary American conservatism is individual liberty. It secures a rational principle first illuminated and defended by thinkers, not religious or social authorities, and established politically by revolution, not custom. This radicalism poses special difficulties for conservatism's defense of the modest and familiar. These difficulties will come to the fore in this chapter, where I turn to the social and political conditions we require to support individual freedom and use it well. The virtues such as responsibility and toleration that accord with exercising rights advance self-interest, generously understood. Nonetheless, to recognize and cultivate them is not automatic. One must be passionately attached to what is reasonably proper and high to make the most of oneself. But we do not form good judgment about what is excellent without education and discipline. For these to flourish we require moral and spiritual practices that fit with liberal democracy. Religion is crucial among these practices. Indeed, the central religious-political issue in the United States today (as distinguished from questions of faith *per se*) is religion's place in securing and advancing the conditions of liberty, not how far to exercise religious liberty in particular cases.

The tension between liberty and its conditions is not hidden. A typical objection to regimes of liberty is that they diminish excellence in the arts and thought: they harm the institutions we need to realize ethical and spiritual height. Indeed, one difference between the conservatism I am discussing and traditional conservatism (even in its American forms) is traditional conservatism's greater emphasis on religion, neighborhood, history, and family. My discussion about virtue moves toward such conservatism, however, just as it moves away from the libertarianism that is its other extreme. My aim in this chapter is to discuss the place and importance of these other elements of conservatism, but from the standpoint of natural rights, liberal virtues, and natural goods.

Institutions

Although virtue belongs to individuals, we cannot achieve or develop it independently from others. It requires not merely random others, moreover, and not even one's family alone, but, also, concrete effort and training—life within schools, churches, the military, businesses, and so on. These institutions operate at least partly by formal and informal authority. Without strong families, education, and religious observance, we will not develop virtue, liberty's use may be vulgar, and we will misunderstand the scope and bearing of equal rights. Family, education, and religion, moreover, are not merely means to liberty and character. They are also fields or venues for dignity and elevation, homes for virtue, places where good things are enjoyed.

The difficulty countries grounded in liberty face is that liberty seems to weaken such institutions. This is so for several reasons. One is that choice makes institutional relations voluntary. It therefore diminishes the implicit or emotional attachments that connect one to religions, traditions, rituals, and localities. Voluntarism means the dominance of the individual who stands outside institutions and selects them, rather than the life lived primarily inside them. One element of the special importance of family is that it is less prone to this voluntarism, although still affected by it.

In addition to this, individual liberty counters institutions' authority. Non-legal authority suggests implicit obedience, but individual liberty rests uneasily with implicit obedience. The voluntary nature of institutions allows us to avoid them if their authority is unpleasant. If we are concerned about them we will never join, demand change and relaxation of rules, leave, or form alternatives. One could consider here the development of religious sects in the United States.[1]

Market economies exacerbate these facts through their relentless change, dependence on individual contracts, and the progressive urbanization that marginalizes small towns and disrupts neighborhood continuity. In addition, liberal democracy's connection to individual property and material rewards results in a bias toward privacy rather than society, a bias away from organized social life, standards, and mores. This direction toward individual satisfaction also leads to smaller families or, indeed, diminished concern with marriage and family. In general, then, liberty favors the voluntary, novel, and individual, rather than the dutiful, traditional, and common.

Worries that traditional institutions, practices, and mores are dissolving, concerns that religion, neighborhood, family, schools, and respect for authority are fading, and fears that the rhythms and practices of everyday life will disappear and the richness embedded in the simple will evaporate motivate much of the twentieth century's resurgence of arguments that favor traditional conservatism. It is not easy to separate the love of liberty from such concerns.

Of course, these dissolving tendencies take time to develop. Their fullest difficulties are not always visible or visible now. Moreover, to restrict liberty in order to enforce authority— the obvious traditional response to these concerns—is hardly an unmixed blessing. As I said in my introduction, many traditional institutions involve unequal, unmerited privilege, deep class divisions, and economic constriction. The attempt to buttress these practices also sometimes involves a cult of violence, moreover, especially once new racial or cultural "nobility" replaces actual warrior ancestors. Some twentieth-century attempts to reaffirm traditional daily ways were fascistic, or associated with Fascism.

Contemporary liberalism also tries to deal with the dissolution of institutions. Its attempts range from highlighting the loss of community to more illiberal discussions, where worries about the integrity or identity of groups lead to excessive distance from the freedom of individuals.[2]

This excessive distance takes the form of permitting or suggesting illiberal practices such as group control of education, freedom for some ethnic or religious groups from certain strictures of liberal life, or wishes to channel resources to these groups to distribute to their members. We see as well demands for tolerance of groups that is actually active support of them.[3] Intellectuals' professional skepticism about Christianity gives way to openness toward Islam. The old worry about small or otiose ultra right-wing groups is replaced by attempts to secure privileges for favored communities.

That these suggestions stem from views of tolerance often not shared by those to whom one applies them seems not to be a matter of concern. The fact that to support conditions which secure narrow ethnic and religious groups is to benefit "leaders" (who are often the very paternalists otherwise condemned) at the expense of individuals who wish to be free or who should enjoy the opportunity to be free seems not enough to change these liberals' illiberal recommendations. What is dominant in such views is fear (as in Western Europe), sentimentality about lives one would never choose for oneself and those one loves, and lack of a secure intellectual base from which to defend liberty and rights.

Liberal concerns about the fate of institutions also involve more benign worries about community. In some cases the worries are close to that of the conservative liberalism I am exploring. In others, however, the motivation involves a wish to expand substantive equality or an effort to enforce sacrifice and public service.

The central difference in this instance (as in others) is whether we conceive individuals primarily as individuals or, rather, as members. When we conceive ourselves as individuals, we seek to build community from individual liberty and virtue and look to institutions to help. We consider the interrelationships among liberty, good character, and authority in their mutual support, but exercising our rights well is central. We are therefore much less tempted by the policy recommendations of community-longers—measures to restrict competition and equalize income (as opposed to sensible taxation and philanthropy), measures to finance campaigns publicly and to restrict deliberation and discussion so that the wealthy are not advantaged and politics is not partisan, measures to demand national or even public service (as opposed merely to promote them), and measures that look to shelter particular communities from ordinary economic development or from "globalism." What happens in these cases is that preserving authorities and traditions becomes an end in itself—forced charity, say, rather than charitable deductions.

To understand more firmly the truth and limits to the concerns I am discussing, we should consider more carefully the nature of institutions and their link to authority. Our goal is to say enough about how institutions work to be able to understand liberty's own resources for conserving what is good in them, and the limits to these resources.

What One Takes for Granted

I am arguing that liberty's basis in individual authority does not mean that regimes of liberty can succeed only as a series of voluntary and contractual actions among individuals. Even the presence of responsibility cannot simply replace the authority of moral, cultural, or social institutions.

A central reason for this is that free choice cannot succeed except within arenas of prejudgment, or matters that we take for granted. These arenas embed our expectations about and in this way secure the future meaning of tasks, careers, families, and the predictability of law. Practical judgment and responsible action require them.

These arenas are first given by what is authoritative. The security of context and the predictability of action are connected to authorities that keep a horizon for judgment in place and manage it—the authority of church, parents, schools, elders, professionals, and government. Trust, reliability, dependability, and predictability appear to require stability that is inseparable from deference. This deference may be rationally defensible but it is not as such rationally experienced. Can one responsibly use individual rights without the institutions they depend on? And, if not, how can one restore or protect deference or its equivalent when voluntary liberalism does so much to dissolve it—often properly?

The growing fragility and increasingly short life of the practices and institutions whose forms we take for granted and in which we base our expectations is significant. So too is decline in the rational content—the virtue and excellence—that they embody. Consider, for example, much of what we teach in secondary schools and colleges, and the flimsy boundary between entertainment and vulgarity. Expectations are worthwhile if they are reasonable. Violating this requirement restricted the worth of many social authorities in the past. For, these authorities often embodied arbitrary and unfair practices.

The economic and social change that accompanies liberal democratic life causes some of the fragility in our institutions and expectations. But much also arises from misinterpreting and enlarging rights. This misinterpretation weakens the link between work, responsibility, and accountability, and expands group entitlements. Such misunderstanding (which, for example, distorts what we expect from the family, how we are permitted to teach, and how we punish) is a central problem. Overweening general law, moreover, much of which stems from this misinterpretation, warps many implicit local, individual, and traditional judgments by forcing them to second-guess themselves legally. But we cannot be successful if we need to calculate everything at each moment. Constant calculation, moreover, counters the steadiness of enjoyment. Substituting method for judgment, law for compromise, and command for love can have only limited success. We cannot wholly replace the worth of the particular with the general. So, although the dominance of natural rights and the rapid economic change they advance surely weaken localities, local knowledge, and some of what is implicit in the enjoyments of everyday life, we exacerbate these difficulties when we understand liberty incorrectly. A proper understanding allows us better to enjoy its fruits.

Institutional "Solutions"

Grounds exist on which to counter the fragility of liberal democracy's institutions while also countering authority's tendency to become irrational and narrow. For, the reasonableness and longevity of the expectations that direct, say, family and work, and direct us to them, is connected to their being natural. Family is especially crucial because it is connected to so many other conserving practices. The natural reasonableness of some authoritative ways stems from their possible excellence (their capacity to elevate us), their shaping of our attachments, and their meeting necessities. Intrusive government and technology make neighborhood, many skills, and even family less necessary, however, and one cannot sensibly create false institutional needs or, at least, trust someone who tries to do so. What we can reasonably hope is to nourish the natural impetus to elevation and attachment even when necessity diminishes. We make institutions' capacity to elevate us concrete through education and the growth of character. Responsibility can actively preserve height and stability in our expectations and practices; together with good education it can be a conserving and elevating principle. We might also hope that responsibility, together with less intrusive government, will permit and to a degree require the freedom of action that produces institutions that mimic sensible community, if not authority simply. We might then further expect that spontaneous attachments and reordering will arise together with the fading of old orders and neighborhoods, something we see regularly with religions and with today's developing and securing of friendships, even across distances. In a regime where we do so much for ourselves, the key is to want to make the best of and choose well for ourselves.

So, the natural elevation and attachment that are embedded in and nurtured by marriage, family, and religion, together with private virtue and action emboldened by diminished government, together with an intellectual class, some of whom support what raises people beyond themselves, may, in varied and somewhat unpredictable ways, advance and encourage the trust and stability that accords with our root individual freedom. One should not be more directive or predictive than this. Those most concerned with communal issues offer no better solutions—and theirs, such as they are, unduly restrict liberty.

The Spirit

Another typical liberal objection to conservatism is to its anti-intellectualism and populist vulgarity. People who vote for conservatives and favor limited government lack or destroy refinement, it is said, and ignore evidence and argument. They enjoy guns, doubt heated claims about global warming, and listen without (sufficient) irony to country music. They occlude and diminish excellence of the mind.

Above all, many take religion seriously, not (only) as useful or habitual, but as true. Such irrationality and its attendant unease with enlightenment and with unchecked license for artist and scientists is, for conservatism's opponents and some of its potential adherents, a central difficulty.

This concern exists despite much of current liberalism's seeming contempt for enlightenment generally. One wonders why intellectuals so confidently expect or desire the disappearance of religion when they attack so fully the reasonable enlightenment grounds for limiting it politically. In any event, religion shows, for them, how conservative talk of individual liberty and responsibility often gives way to concrete controls whose origin is religious moralism, or populist fear.

We can counter these objections, while still leaving as a residue what remains forceful in them. As we are arguing, conservatism that conserves liberal democratic principles supports political communities based on reason. The United States is formed to serve the principles that are developed by John Locke and his philosophical predecessors and successors, announced by the Declaration of Independence, and made politically concrete by a Constitution formed by deliberation and discussion. The principles of our conservatism are not irrational but, on the contrary, are primarily the rational principles of the Enlightenment.

Of course, despite what I have claimed about enlightenment, one might say that conservatives question scientific education. It is not liberals who believe in intelligent design. Indeed, liberals' main evidence for conservative irrationalism is religion. Conservatives frighten liberals because many actually seem to believe. Or, some of their policy judgments are fueled by belief.

Religion

Religion has normally belonged to what conservatives seek to conserve. Traditional conservatives seek to secure particular practices and, therefore, particular religious practices. In the United States these practices are primarily Christian. Remarkably, they are also coordinated with tolerance. More broadly, our religious life accords with the revolutionary and constitutional principles to which toleration belongs.

The dominance of toleration does not mean, nor was it intended by the American founders to require, the disappearance of religion. Rather, toleration makes religion chiefly a private or voluntary matter. Moreover, it means that Christianity itself, and much of Judaism, are increasingly interpreted in ways that allow them to be compatible with individual rights, responsible action, and equal opportunity to acquire. They are significant in advancing moral and intellectual culture.

Despite religion's private status in our country, belief is sometimes the proximate cause of political action. This is not surprising. For all their compatibility with energetic freedom, moreover, many Protestant, Catholic, and Jewish believers defend policies that in some areas limit free action. Differences in the scope of free action obviously split libertarian from religious conservatives. Political battles, of course, must still be fought politically. Indeed, on what are arguably the two major religiously influenced issues of the past forty years, abortion and gay marriage, it is the secular, not the religious, view that led the way in constraining legislative freedom by seeking to enshrine its preference judicially.

Most conservatives believe not just that our dominant religions are good as such but that they support liberty, good character, and general spiritual uplift. In fact, almost everyone is still surprised or especially disturbed by immorality and crudeness among religious leaders. And, one recalls the link between the Catholic Church (and some early Protestantism) and fine music and art. Despite our cynicism, the likely or possible link between religion and excellence is easily enough remembered and understood.

If believers are correct, religion and conservatism are indeed compatible. Conserving religion will help prevent us from sliding into the vague socialism and self-absorption to which the irreligious Europeans have tumbled. But perhaps "religion" is too broad a term. Conservatives are not partisans of polytheism, ritual sacrifice, or radical Islam. Not long ago, in fact, many conservatives were less than delighted with Jews and many Catholics, and with those Protestant sects to which they did not belong. Recently, however, beginning in the 1950s and expanding from the 1970s on, the growth of more fundamentalist Protestantism, more orthodox Catholicism, and a friendlier attitude toward Judaism and Israel began to walk hand in hand with conservative politics.

One reason for the diminution of battles among such groups is the similarity of their secular concerns. Not merely tolerance or the general ecumenism of liberal Protestantism but a likeness in anti-Communism, in promotion of individual choice and self-reliance (responsibility), in dislike of corruption and moral rot, and in worries about the family and abortion led to alliance, or mutual support.

From our perspective, the crux is that these specific religious beliefs or their secular manifestations apparently support the conservative version of liberal democracy. Much traditional American faith admires the original structure and understanding of rights within whose ambit faith grows. The public virtue of religion is toleration, not orthodoxy, but the views and practices of many denominations help to conserve liberty. Religion that is politically under the aegis of natural rights can and often does support them, even if privately the full scope of the doctrines or hopes of some sects may wish to limit or direct them.

There are several reasons for this coordination of faith and liberty: the dominance of private choice and life that allows faith and observance to be an important part of the whole but not the whole; the coordination between freedom generally and freedom to worship; the fear of tyrannies that control, direct, or limit religion; the connection of religion to the human soul understood as voluntary and free; the difference between virtue, patriotism, and mere materialism, and religion's dislike of simple materialism; the implicit understanding of the individual worshipper as the modern individual; and the dominance of the power of modern liberty so that it colors religion and faith.[4]

Religion and Liberty

The mutual support of liberty and religion allows both to flourish in each others' presence. But, no one sensible could say that this flourishing is guaranteed. My point, rather, is that this support can and does exist.[5] It is true that this coalescing favors particular religious interpretations and that it is connected to the attempt from Locke forward to show that Christianity is reasonable because it accords with natural rights and their ground. The fact that these interpretations needed to be wrested from the reigning Christianity, however, does not mean that they are false.

To put this in another way, religion, or the belief in what is divine and just, belongs to human recognition of our own height and dignity. Reverence, awe, and the sanctifying of birth, marriage, and death help to secure and express human dignity and inviolability. Equal natural rights belong to and help define the secular truth of the soul with such passions. We can see belief in the divine and just as a way to respond to the fact of our equal self-direction, and to our ability to choose what is high, within the possibility of natural truth. Moral education and at least the start of intellectual education, moreover, require habit, tradition, authority, and even reverence—elevation expressed and secured in what one takes for granted. Religion can help to establish this height.

Views on policy and law that restrict license can certainly arise from religious belief even when it is largely in accord with individual freedom and the virtues that support it. This is unsurprising, and often desirable. Especially with abortion, the limits demanded are often connected to the height from which freedom is defended. Whether the view from faith wins politically is decided in the political arena. But there is also a private or social realm where faith defends liberty as inviolability, and each human as an object of respect. This defense will and has had significant effect. Conservatism is "culture" or opinion and the institutions they shape, as well as law.

To think that even religious belief that prizes reason will never demand the disagreeable would be foolish. Many have unpleasant memories of religious education and ritual, or do not seem to need it to establish virtue and respect. It is also obvious that religious belief can become intolerant when powerful or publicly authoritative. And, as I have indicated, not everything that calls itself religious respects reason. Nonetheless, the ways I have outlined in which religion, individual rights, and limited government can offer mutual support are clear.

The current danger in the relation between religion and freedom is not that American religion is illiberal: the independent soul and moral virtue are seen largely to accord with individual rights and responsibility. The danger, rather, is that our religion will fade in importance, to be replaced by selfish materialism or illiberal religion—what we see in Europe and much of Islam. That religion can help conserve liberty does not mean that regimes of liberty always help to conserve religion.

The obvious dangers are visible abroad and in declining church and synagogue attendance here, despite the over 90% of Americans who claim to believe in God.[6] This claim is remarkable. But, can it survive a decline in ritual, the press of the material, vulgarity, variety, mobility, and the possible decline of the family? Can faith survive modern physics, biology, and chemistry? When belief preserves, represents, and inspires to what is naturally reasonable and high, it has reason's protection, whatever natural science discovers. When faith supports and is supported by responsibility and other liberal virtues, and intellectual leaders see it in its true power, belief and liberty strengthen each other. Still, one wonders how religion can remain powerful if we do not observe it in its daily rituals and details.

Music and Art

The attack on supposed conservative irrationalism also takes the form of decrying the vulgarity or mediocrity of liberal democratic art and music. This criticism is heard less than it once was, but is perhaps increasingly valid nonetheless. One objection to regimes of equal liberty is that they weaken the conditions of leisure, culture, and high aspiration that are vital to spiritual excellence. To conserve liberty is to conserve mediocrity, or so it is thought.

This dominance of mediocrity, one might reply, cannot exclusively or primarily be blamed on those who preserve equal liberty. It is furthered today by egalitarianism, multicultural excess, and disbelief in the reasonable defense of equal rights. These standpoints result from today's liberals. Our vast diversity does leave room for excellence, moreover; the difficulty is not that excellence is fading but that it has decreasing influence over culture generally.

Liberty and Mediocrity: The Argument

The source of the argument that links liberty to mediocrity is both theoretical and empirical. How could a devotion to equality, even as equal rights, protect and develop the inequality vital for excellence? How could materialism advance the spirit? From where could arise the necessary devotion and training?[7]

The empirical argument simply asks one to look around. Especially from the founding of the United States until the first or even the second world war, who would not say that our art and music were inferior to the products of less democratic Europe?

One might counter this empirical argument in several ways. One is that these claims conveniently ignore natural science, not merely as the source of technology but as a mode of thought. And it is liberal democracies that spearhead scientific thought. The counterclaims that liberal regimes are now not the only homes of science and that it is now more a matter of group than of individual effort do not eliminate the presence of enormous individual scientific and mathematical excellence in liberal democracies. Perhaps these efforts once justified themselves solely as serving business and defense, but they now have life and power of their own. A second reply concerns beauty—music and the arts. There is surely more access to refined music and art than there once was, with every city worshipping its museums, supporting music, and housing artists, and especially, musicians, who have remarkable technical skills.

In reply, one suggests that whatever the technical skills the substance of today's art and music, especially what we newly produce, is declining. Contemporary art is trivial or outlandish, and contemporary music is gimmicky, shallowly repetitive of older styles, or unlistenable. Support for fine music is in fact weakening.

A reply to this is that any decline in fine music and art is largely a matter of passing taste. Just as fine music recovered from atonal excess and architecture from the dominance of the unembellished and the ugly, so too will art and music assert and continue to reassert finer forms. Fine art will continue to exist in strength despite the surrounding cacophony and ebbs and flows of opinion.

This leads one to suggest next that whatever the empirical and theoretical overstatements about the decline of excellence it is at least true that although the excellent may survive it is surrounded and dwarfed by the vulgar and unrefined. It is at most the private interest of a few, and when some piece of art or artist becomes a sensation or a celebrity, it is quickly vulgarized and its true rank ignored. The issue is not so much the disappearance of the excellent as its unimportance in the way of life fostered by liberty.

Of course, truly grasping the excellent may always have been the preserve only of the few, although it seems that the "popular" was often deeper than it is now, more directly influenced by the excellent, or itself excellent.[8] The true issue is that the few no longer form the culture but are only one segment among many. The result is that the fine, even if we continue to recognize it, will fade, at least to the degree that it needs the support of the whole.

But to what degree is this? Need the support be more than our general freedom of action combined with wealth? The spread of wealthy classes across the globe will perhaps be a source of sustenance for the arts or even of demands for (expanded) government funding for them.

On the other hand, current support of the excellent may result more from habit and tradition than from genuine appreciation that is still growing. The issue is not just freedom and wealth, but the training and education of the wealthy. Without separate leisure classes and without cultures that prize the spirit education will weaken and public support will fade. Wealth and freedom will not be enough.

If so, preserving and encouraging the fine and refined may in some areas (say, music) largely be a private, limited, matter. But there is no reason to believe that given the enormous number of private choices and technological possibilities they will disappear altogether. In some areas, indeed, (say, visual art) they may well hold their own. Moreover, training and education need not always remain in their current depression.[9]

Education

Do or must regimes devoted to liberty diminish serious education? The short answer is that they need not, although they do now. They need not because a link exists between liberty and liberal education. Authoritative self-direction suggests that no one blocks me in what I seek, consistent with responsibly securing equal rights. It also suggests that I can see and consider the possible goods I might choose, and that my understanding can grasp the general conditions for which I could take responsibility. Liberty requires more than appropriate lack of external limits and restrictions. It requires an expansive mind if it is to be true self-direction.

For much expansiveness, liberal education is beneficial if not necessary. This is a chief reason why liberty and enlightenment go hand in hand. This union also is meant to decrease the influence of religion and of ascription generally. Liberal education is one cause of the weakening of the implicit power of traditional institutions.

Liberal education and, especially, mass education beyond economic need seems nonetheless to counter excellence precisely because it is so widespread. What could it mean to teach literature or philosophy seriously to so many who are apparently unable to give them the subtle attention they deserve? Moreover, education's tendency to try to be useful seems exacerbated in liberal democracy. The emphasis on material expansion and technology means that advanced education is largely technical—agricultural, commercial, legal, and scientific.

Yet, this emphasis was once compatible with a deep grasp of our political principles. In fact, this grasp seemed to exist even with grammar or secondary education alone. The technically minded founders and the technically minded Lincoln are obviously unsurpassed by anyone today. And even at a more general level, the notion that *The Federalist* was meant to sway votes and be widely read would bemuse or frighten today's political consultants and advisers. By what standards, indeed, could one claim that advanced scientific and economic education in liberal democracies is mediocre? The issue is more with the substance of today's liberal education than with a necessary mediocrity caused by regimes of equal liberty, although the spread of education and the dominance of the material are always significant.

The difficulty with today's substance is linked to the causes of the misunderstanding of rights that I noted in my first chapter. We claim that important matters are historically or culturally variable in their meaning and truth, random results of struggles for power, or inherently and fully relative. With varying degrees of sophistication such views become dominant and affect the teaching and study of history, literature, philosophy, politics, sociology, psychology, and even economics. This historicism distorts our understanding of rights and dissolves the energy we should direct to other important studies. What sensible person would spend time exploring difficult matters or learning to choose what is best if everything significant is a variable matter of accident, opinion, and imposition?

These relativistic views work in tandem with today's liberalism's emphasis on equality, groups, the dispossessed, and the disadvantaged. Their situation is fully undeserved, it is claimed, because they have been overpowered by force and fraud, or because nothing is deserved in any event. Their truths and culture are as true and high as anything else. Given these liberal views one then also understands conservatives' preference for more traditional and serious education.

Despite links between liberal democracy and liberal education, it is wrong to reduce the intellectual to the political or to explain the political solely in terms of the intellectual. One might attempt to conserve excellence in education whatever the politics. Indeed, counter-trends to those I just discussed exist in higher academic life somewhat apart from politics, and one hopes that they will make their way to secondary education, as have the trends they try to meet. Moreover, our concern about diminished literacy and numeracy do not accord with the relativism we otherwise profess.

Excellence

One might wonder what constitutes excellence here. This question is significant beyond education. It goes to the problem of what we choose, of how we best exercise natural rights. Choosing well is a question of virtue and talent but also of traditions, institutions, and expectations. One does not choose to become a professional poker player or entertainment lawyer in the Middle Ages, or even today one if one hates numbers or false bravado. These restrictions, however, do not change the fact that some goods are naturally better to pursue than others or some choices more sensible than others.

"Better" means an orientation toward goods that satisfy and form human powers, directly and indirectly. Something good is useful, beneficial, or helpful; these characteristics are in the end directed to what is fully satisfactory, the best, the excellent. In general, what is good brings out human reason, the passions intelligently organized, and powers such as wonder, laughter, and curiosity, reasonably directed. What is most important to know, most natural, most beautiful, and most just, taken together, is what is best. Our orientation to these excellences and living within them is what is most satisfactory for us.

The substance of such goods is not self-evident. They are disputable in their nature. What, after all, is beauty? Not only are they disputable, they are not always visibly coherent. Is my love for this one and these few simply compatible with just devotion to the country? Nonetheless, such disputes do not obviate the facts of significant, reasonable, direction, and agreement: what is beautiful is some combination of what stands out, elevates, pleases, and fits, whatever the disputes. The philosophical examination of such questions is itself the fullest life, as Plato and Aristotle teach us.

Natural freedom and choice are implicated in enjoying genuine goods. Moreover, the practical reason involved in exercising one's responsibilities (one's tasks as objects of virtue) is substantial. We can therefore experience a general availability and expression of what is good in many of our contemporary satisfactions. This general availability, however, is also shaped today by goods grasped as objects of equal desire and, therefore, by their resultant equivalence in choiceworthiness. How we spend our time is judged permissively and equally. What is common to us are virtues and liberty, but also a certain flatness and sameness in what we enjoy. The difference between more and less wealth results primarily in more of the same goods (more and larger houses, say), not differences in goods' complexity and range.

This equality and flatness of satisfactions—each tends to be understood so that it is available to be purchased or experienced by all—diminishes what is high. We have discussed this with the arts. Here the key point is that formal or intellectual education is central to preserve serious knowledge of some goods beyond this flatness and to direct us toward experiencing them. If we are to conserve excellence it is essential to preserve education as an opening to what is truly good. In fact, this orientation can belong together coherently with a deep or proper understanding of rights. Education is a central place (together with family) where people's hopes can be elevated—something especially vital in a country where serious aspirations, difficult enough to find to begin with, are often directed toward the trivial.

Conserving Excellence in Education

There are no magical ways to overcome the degradation of liberal education, but some measures help. We have attempted them with some success in the past quarter century. Pockets of serious study and scholarship must continue, as they can when enough schools are urged to be serious and supported in their efforts. Government intrusions in speech and selection must be fought at every step. Responsible people must demonstrate the courage of their convictions and take appropriate risks and stands, practically as well as on paper. One must try to keep beachheads in elite institutions and shame those who place excellence under the thumb of politics, or academic narrowness and fashion. Elite institutions, however, are not the only ones where we can find and support fine students and faculty. Special programs should make serious work available to those who lack it in their own schools. Law students and faculty should continue to organize against the dominance of politicized law, and against the dominance of narrow professionalism. The idea in all these measures is to protect serious questioning and examination, to defend the constitutional understanding and practical common sense that should surround law and government, to question the reigning historicism, relativism, and dogmatism, and to grasp the genuine equality and freedom (i.e., of rights) we should protect. It is hard to deal with entrenched academics but hardly impossible.

Excellence is difficult to conserve in any circumstance and liberal democracy poses special challenges to it. These challenges are real but we can navigate among them in the ways I have discussed. In any event, we should recognize how difficult it will always be to advance free, unbridled, questioning—the energy of reason—while also understanding where the limits of political regimes rest, so that we expect neither too much from them nor too little.

CHAPTER FOUR

Conserving Self-Government

If our moral and intellectual situation is disturbing or even perilous, one might wonder why government should stay on the sidelines. If public education is a proper political function, why should there not be other intellectual, moral, and cultural mandates? What, in fact, is government's proper place even in economic regulation? How should it conduct itself where it makes sense for it to intervene? What is the link between natural rights, liberal virtues, and self-government, even if self-government is not always prudent government?

In this chapter I will sketch a standpoint for understanding policy and discuss self-government's merits and necessity. Conservatism's modesty indicates that we can at most employ guidelines for intervention, not use hard and fast rules. I will argue that the chief guideline for legislation and action is to judge, prudently, their overall effects on securing equal liberty, advancing responsible character, and permitting intelligent individual choice. When government must act, moreover, it should not use means that subvert the ends it attempts to serve.

These guidelines should also direct our use of semitechnical standards for judging claims about intervention, such as cost-benefit analysis, and our choices about which effects on others merit political action. Our standpoint suggests vigorous self-government by the people, not remote bureaucratic choice. Self-government results in partisanship, not analytic calm, moreover, so those who love liberty should not fear argument or dispute.

One general way to secure liberty's conditions without subverting it is to look for policy mechanisms that use the very characteristics whose enhancement is their goal. This is why conservatism favors private choice and action even when effecting a government purpose. This standpoint, however, does not solve all tensions among our ends or about government's service to them. It belongs to conservatism to acknowledge the merits of the moderation that stems from recognizing imperfection. A fair look at American conservatism also shows, however, that it wishes above all to conserve our equal freedom, not privileges for the few. We should prefer active, responsible, self-government, moderated by common sense about our limitations.

Self-Government

Conservatives usually discuss self-government less than they do excessive government. Interference in private freedom, especially economic freedom, is the normal concern. Today, however, unease about oppressive interference is often matched or supplemented by worry that we rule ourselves only nominally. Many fear that our powers of self-government are usurped by bureaucrats, experts, private interests, unaccountable representatives, and mysterious and uncontrollable social forces.[1]

The two concerns are in fact connected, because to control excess in government we need self-government by citizens. Mere mechanisms (such as seemingly automatic spending caps) that restrict government can be useful. One could imagine taking control from the people and giving it to administrative-limiters, say a sensible court. But mechanisms are not self-enforcing, and control sooner or later falls into harmful hands. Promises by representatives to do the right thing must be reviewed and tested constantly. As long as freedom exists, to check government requires active self-government.

More than this, self-governing is itself both a cause and a consequence of the responsibility we need to execute our rights successfully. Our virtues and the self-understanding that they realize demand free political action as one of the appropriate fields for their expression.

Although self-government is necessary for government to be both constrained and free, it does not guarantee government that is limited or wise. To increase political participation sometimes means to expand government's size and scope. One reason people involve themselves politically is to increase their benefits and favors. Still, much that encourages self-government today also tends to discourage excessive government. The present world of government benefits and political favors is often, and perhaps mostly, a world of administrative regulation and hidden legislation. In any event, how to protect and expand self-government while also advancing limited government is always a practical dilemma without an automatic solution.

Is Self-Government Declining?

To advance our discussion we should explore more carefully why people think that self-government is diminishing. Scholars and pundits usually defend this claim by mentioning low electoral turnout rates and citizens' startlingly high disapproval of political institutions.[2] They explain these by pointing to the corrosive effects of negative campaign advertising, the caustic effects of vitriolic political rhetoric, and the corrupting effects of excessive campaign spending. So many candidates and representatives are now partisan extremists, one further claims, that the average citizen is alienated from politics.[3]

A second worry points more to administration than to politics. The tangle of government's rules and regulations is so complex that it is beyond timely escape for anyone caught in it. The public employees who make the rules and the judges who interpret them appear isolated from the concerns of those they serve. Even when we see local action that responds to citizens' desires, it is regularly trumped by federal interference—the interference of distant, unjust, ideologically driven, or corrupt officials. Moreover, this complexity, distance, imposition, and venality encourage unfair political favoritism and arbitrary redistribution of wealth.

These, in turn, cause still further government excess. The result is that self-government is severely constrained.

Partisanship

I believe that the first set of concerns largely misunderstands what intelligent and limited self-government requires. Low turnout and easy cynicism about political institutions are not especially grave problems. Why should one want rule by those too lazy or selfish to vote? Why should one want the dominance by redistributors that strict control of wealth in campaigns would most likely advantage? Much law that tries to correct electoral troubles adds to them by restricting political freedom. Policies that exacerbate the problem they are addressing through the solutions they offer are foolish.

Perhaps the deepest issue here is a mistake about partisanship, and the view that harsh words about opponents and their opinions are out of bounds. Partisanship strikes many people as problematic, and this is true if the partisanship is so extreme that its source or goal is outside the order that protects individual rights. But middling and soft agreement within the confines of the regime will not always discover the common good. Nor is it fully desirable or possible, given the nature of liberty. From the conservative point of view, no partisanship, or no partisanship that strikes Democrats as extreme, means no Reagan, or no effective opposition to Obama's excesses.

The power of non-partisanship is visible in people's dislike of parties and wish that politicians serve the common good. We expect common action if our boundaries and principles are attacked. The obvious example is war. But being partisan usually belongs to the competitive genius of successful free government. It helps check the complete control or monopoly that many leaders—other "partisans"—want. It helps limit political action to areas where agreement is broad enough that partisanship within it is acceptable, for example, helping to generate wealth. And, it helps to correct government misdeeds. Why, after all, should Republicans acquiesce in Democrats' unrestraint or Democrats in Republicans'? No one is pleased when the wish to win leads to blatant distortion. But to eliminate partisanship, or to see everything one dislikes as impermissibly beyond the pale is harmful. Accusations of overheated rhetoric and scurrilous campaigning usually strike partisans as—partisan. Indeed, although mudslinging in electioneering can damage decency, it cannot hide for long campaigners' characters and views. What we need, from the standpoint of conserving liberty, is partisanship within the limits of our way of life. Nothing should or ultimately does prevent a free people from being politically energetic, useful, and active, as popular movements show us again and again. The proper degree of (informal) restriction on partisan rhetoric is something that voters must establish by rewarding what they desire.[4]

Elites

The more significant facts about declining self-government, and its deeper causes, involve the distance from the people of our governors, and the complexity of the rules, regulations, and procedures that they construct for us. One cause of this distance is the excessive attraction of government, law, the academy, and the media as professions. An often overlooked virtue of liberal democracy is the room it makes for spirited enterprise. This spirit involves not just ordinary politics but the existence of entrepreneurs, "captains of industry," and competition among them. We satisfy and limit not only economic but also political passions by the kind of energy and responsibility that starts, forms, and directs organizations, and, in particular, businesses.

When this possibility is constrained as it is increasingly for us, and when so much talent is oriented to law, government, media, and the academy, self-government declines for two reasons. One is the economic stagnation that presses upon us government action that is increasingly restrictionist and redistributionist. A second, perhaps more subtle reason, is that "success" in areas such as government and the academy is not won through economic competition, often involves criticism, carping, and "justifying" one's views apart from any real price to be paid for error, and usually involves expanding government. These fields tend to foster vague responsibility for the whole rather than concrete responsibility for a few. Their growing attraction for the talented is one of the forces that gives America, and especially its elites, an increasingly illiberal, European, feel.

To the degree that the media and law are businesses they create their own empires—media empires as we say. But both, and law in particular, are economically draining rather than productive. And, law and, especially, the academy and bureaucracy produce figures who fancy themselves to be the last word, not part of an ever-competitive word. Contemporary success in the areas of many with talent increasingly points away from productive competition and, thus, diminishes the competitive, private, political energy that is vital for self-government that also wishes to limit government.

Government's Scope

The central requirement in advancing self-government is to reduce government's scope and size, and the number and complexity of issues with which it deals. This reduction diminishes the everyday stakes of politics and reorients government to large, central issues. This reorientation permits focused attention and direction even without a specialist's expertise. And, of course, limiting government is useful in its own right.

But how can we obtain this reduction, given the remoteness of government from so many? How, especially, can we obtain it given the prevalence and dominance of experts, bureaucrats, and judges?

Two phenomena are worth remarking. One is that however much specialized knowledge expands we can still control government's direction because we can know whether it conforms to reasonable ends, principles, and balances among them. Experts see these ends no better than do other citizens. The second is that common sense and practical reason can place expert advice within a sensible context, and evaluate it.

To understand our ends is to grasp correctly our broad aims of freedom, virtue, and excellence and more immediate goals such as security and health. Public debate is often about the meaning, rank, and relationship of these ends. How much security of what sort should be risked by how much freedom of speech, care in trials, privacy in activity, and so on. How much health is worth how much funding? How much equality is worth how much excellence? How much safety is worth how much local control? How much military might is worth how much money? How much short-term economic difficulty is worth how much attention to the long term?

These are questions that technical experts as such cannot answer. They are not mere matters of opinion, however, for we can discuss them reasonably. From a common sense standpoint voters and representatives are adequate to grasp what the proper political goals should be, adequate to understand the effects of actions on ends, and adequate to see the fit among our goals.

Such adequacy does not mean perfect or equal understanding. Its source is to comprehend how equal rights and limited, constitutional, government are connected. The major difficulty is not that liberty's principles are abstruse, but that expertise is so powerful in its claims and in its mechanisms of legalistic and scientific analysis that common sense discussion and evaluation seems very difficult. The counter to this is education about, and government directed to, equal liberty and the character that advances it. We need a people and representatives who seek to conserve our founding liberties.

Guidelines for Governing

Given this standpoint, what guidelines can we use to make choices and propose laws? What directions should we keep in mind? I do not suggest that these guidelines make choice easy. Their number and complexity indicate government's difficulty. And, any choice here and now depends on judging circumstances. Where will I find the money, votes, and public support I need? Nonetheless, guidelines give direction and limit harm.

The first consideration is to ask whether a proposal promotes freedom and virtue, whatever other need it meets, and then to see whether (when relevant) its mechanisms use the virtues and freedoms it tries to enhance. After all, the central goal of government should be to help allow people to do important things for themselves.

This guideline does not go far in limiting areas where government may act. It suggests, rather, how it might act, and its intention to leave people alone, where it can. What is central is to protect the spirit and right to do things for oneself, not advance a theory of what must always or never be a public good or promote formulae for intervention that are in fact easy to distort.

The most obviously useful government actions are well-enforced rules that control crime, cheating, and unfairness but do not distort initiative, infrastructure that is better provided publicly than privately, and defense against enemies. But if people are going to be able to do things for themselves we also need a level of access to education, open markets, and property that is sufficiently high to control the effects of inequality so they do not warp the effective use of rights.

The obvious but sometimes overlooked example of an arena that uses the virtues and freedoms it tries to enhance is the market, where we support private action because it is a site of freedom, responsibility, and justly equal access, not only because it is more productive than social control. We find other examples in some recent social policy, where we use as a means several of the capabilities we wish to enhance. School choice and tenant management of public housing come to mind, as do enhancing individual responsibility for retirement and health care. It helps in these cases that health, wealth, and learning are as well or better provided by choice and competition as by mandate. In fact, it is never wise to underestimate how many government services we can provide competitively.

This picture has three blemishes to which we should attend. Although we want to enhance freedom and responsibility in helping to provide health, wealth, and learning because securing freedom and its virtues is our truest political end, we also want to advance health, wealth, and learning themselves. When government mandates primary and secondary education, it has in mind subjects to be learned at a certain level; when it regulates pharmaceuticals or funds Medicaid, it has in mind health to be provided that meets certain standards. It is wrong to ignore how far competition may lift service, but it is foolish to think that improvement must occur inevitably. The incentives to monopolize and misinform are present in all areas and one cannot be certain that everyone will demand goods at the level of education or even health that responsible freedom should seek. Professional responsibility, internal policing, and competition cannot meet all issues in a timely way.

This also suggests that we should understand liberty's preference for private action prudently, not ideologically. It is a habit of those who prefer government to contrast a pure or idealized public with private venality—nobly disinterested and competent environmental regulators with air polluting criminals. It is a habit of those who prefer private action to contrast a pure or idealized market with government at its worst—eager technical innovators producing brighter and brighter bulbs at lower and lower costs with dim, expensive, mandated bulbs produced by a favored few.[5] Instead, we should compare honest versions of government and markets when we defend the benefits of free choice.

We also should be prudent about the need to preserve what we habitually take for granted as a backdrop against which novelty and choice are useful. Perhaps it is better if everyone does not need to make a thousand investment decisions or if there is a guaranteed base—better not always in terms of wealth itself, but in terms of the overall economy of life, of the balance of leisure and necessity. One should ask how important it is in any situation to enhance choice rather than conditions of security and excellence.

The second consideration concerns necessity. Free countries must protect themselves domestically and abroad. Security sometimes requires urgent action. Disasters sometime require urgent measures. Urgency requires rapid political response. Purity of method is less important than quick results. Advance planning can limit government imposition, and it is good to leave behind as little imposition as possible. But the goals of a free county depend on its safety, stability, and prosperity. Conservatism is principled but not moralistic in its wish to limit government. One cannot always meet immediate necessity with the same means one uses to develop beyond it. In fact, for the foreseeable future a strong link will exist between conserving liberty and American strength. This link will demand anticipation of urgency and an effort to assist current and future friends that will lead to larger government than conservatives otherwise prefer.

A third consideration concerns technical as opposed to common sense knowledge. As I indicated above, self-government is constrained to the degree that governing is a matter of expertise. How can one actually subject expert knowledge to the standpoint of advancing freedom's ends and goals?

The beginning point for a representative or citizen is to consider whether technical knowledge must really have its head. In what ways are the issues technical? How much do they involve means, not ends? How accurate is the technical understanding? How much do experts genuinely disagree?

The military trains senior officers to understand technical possibilities sufficiently to grasp their military worth. It trains them to manage weapons production and implementation. No one sensible would say that producing and purchasing weapons should be a simple free-for-all or altogether subject to democratic vote. Yet, specialized weapons-knowledge leaves us vulnerable to overstatement by the military (and to it). Overstatement exists because weapons purchases answer to political and service rivalry, not only to central plans, which are sometimes unreasonable in any event.[6] So, we do not in fact leave all choice about research and weapons development to the military and its contractors.

The common sense or political guidelines here concern judging the relative importance of military to other spending, and knowing that recognizing threats and preparing for them are political matters, not merely technical ones. Other guidelines applicable here (and in other matters) are: knowing that freedom and competition are useful scientifically whomever is doing the spending; knowing that the direct line of supervisors (here, the military) must be habituated and directed in the public good; knowing that proposers of products will often overstate their merits; trusting experts who agree with you on other issues, while testing that trust through broader reading and consultation; and distrusting claims of expertise that are not based on truly technical matters.

One might compare military to economic experts. Here too these general guidelines help to manage technical claims. It is especially important to ask whether genuine conflict exists among experts and, if so, which group of competing policies will allow the greatest freedom of action and least favoritism. It is often hard to know how broad expert conflict is (human contribution to global warming is an example) but one can know enough to measure the effects of proposals against the likelihood of outcomes. In scientific and medical research the question is how to allocate funds in terms of the importance of their goals and likelihood of success, and what limits to put on the research, publicly and even privately. All these are matters of political judgment, including serious attention to scientists' claims. Such judgment depends on grasping and ranking our ends and fitting them together.

Localism

A final general question concerns localism. Many conservatives believe that we should treat political and social questions at the smallest or lowest level that can do the job, the family, the neighborhood, the town, the city, the state. This preference is linked to federalism and to the standpoint of subsidiarity.[7] And, it is connected to individual liberty, which grounds choice at a still more elementary level.

Several difficulties exist with this position. One is that the local level may still be very broad. Many state governments are as remote from citizens as is the national government— more remote in a way because usually less observed by the media. This is true to a degree of city governments too, and of the many overlapping districts that so confusingly manage local affairs. Transparency and greater knowledge, and, therefore, more informed control do not automatically favor localism.

Localities may also be more overbearing than larger units or effectively less free. They can be dominated by small cliques, by the few rich and powerful, by narrow majorities. Big-city ideas may corrupt small town youth, but small towns are sometimes stultifying. In fact, it is often larger governments that must control the corruption of smaller ones.[8] And, larger rather than smaller communities are sometimes the vehicles of the universal principles of equal rights that stem from individual reason and choice. Although, as I have argued, small institutions are often the home for good practices that we take for granted, they can also be the home for unjust ones. The appeal to broad principle, the orientation to universal culture, can liberate, and it primarily liberates individuals. We do not allow families complete control of children's education.[9]

Localism also fails to tell us how much government we need to begin with, and where. Local government, indeed, is not necessarily small government, but may be overweening government, advancing, say, constricting school curricula or economic monopolies. Courts with broad jurisdiction may defend individuals better than their own small towns.[10] I conclude, therefore, that although a local orientation is often sensible because truly small venues allow greater practical understanding of interests and circumstances, it is not always one that favors individual freedom.

Summary

The ways to conserve self-government are to favor: free, responsible private action, not public control; partisanship, not false consensus; political representatives, not experts and officials; skepticism about claims that a problem needs technical solutions; engaged patriotism and professional limits, not narrow vision or professional excess; and a healthy understanding of the link between American primacy and the primacy of liberty.

Liberty and Practical Understanding

I will approach our conclusion by discussing more fully than I have to this point the connections among liberty, practical reason, and common sense. To conserve liberty we must advance the virtues with which we use our rights. Seeing things responsibly and courageously is primarily a matter of practical reasoning, not technical skill. Estimating the connected effect of our actions on liberty is also largely a matter of practical vision. To conserve liberty, therefore, is to conserve the scope of practical reason. This requires that we explore and understand it.

We discussed in the third chapter conservative concern about the decline of neighborhoods, institutions, religious life, and authority. A fear animates much traditional conservatism that we live in a world where human effort, self-reliance, and the importance of ordinary competence are diminishing. Much everyday life involves practical action connected to experience: practical reason is vital in the way institutions work. Tensions surely exist between ordinary expectations and the universality of equal rights but, as we suggested, natural freedom and its virtues can also support our attachments and best expectations. We will also understand this issue better by exploring practical understanding.

I will begin by looking at practical knowledge, and then focus on the connection between practical reason and responsibility, our broadest modern virtue.

Practical Knowledge

The first thing to notice is that when people act practically, their understanding is tied to a purpose. They intend to win a battle, prevent crime, persuade other legislators, or sell a suit.[11] Their goal is not knowledge for its own sake. Their standard and direction comes from serving their ends, not from following a method, as with technical knowledge. Practical knowing, moreover, is intrinsic in activities: the usual legislator or policeman is involved in a hands-on effort in which he persuades and commands. Indeed, practical knowledge usually belongs to shaping the event in which it is gaining and deploying understanding. The correct outcome is not given fully in advance, to be calmly observed. Such knowledge is also particular knowledge because active situations often differ individually.

The next thing to see is that practical knowledge is limited. A police officer cannot know with certainty that someone sitting in a parked blue car is hiding illegal narcotics. Of course, few things are clearer than that someone is now sitting in that blue car. What we know practically is not always disputed. Yet, that the person sitting in the blue car seems suspicious, or that someone will stand by his negotiating position, is reasonably disputable. Why? Because, when we judge suspicion, we must speak and listen as well as look and see. Fraud then becomes easy: lying is one obstacle to practical certainty.

Context

Ascertaining whether actions are suspicious is also disputable because we need to group and separate them with a name—"suspicious." This requires a background or context to stand out. Indeed, context is central in much practical understanding and action. It involves recent actions, what we normally recognize about purpose and order, and the next set of actions that we expect or see. Declarations that one will vote against a bill have different force if the vote is the one that counts, or merely a step along the way. Context affects whether behavior is suspicious much more than it affects whether a car looks blue. The greater the importance of context, the less obviously certain are practical statements.[12]

The elements in a context that are reasonably subject to dispute sometimes help us to grasp it. But recognizing the context often centers on what is disputable about it—a sense one has of the end, goal, or whole order before it is announced, or an implicit weaving of clues to confirm, develop, or reach a deeper view of the whole. We cannot build up the context from separate, meaningless, factors; rather, we must grasp ends and intentions together with actions that look appropriate or inappropriate. Seeing a bulge as a dangerous gun follows from first seeing the context. Understanding the political meaning or import of an economic report or proposal that presents itself as merely technical or neutral often depends on seeing the context. So, although practical action deals with particulars, the specifics are inseparable from the generality that gives them meaning. This is why talk about level of threat and prior history is important when we deal with terrorism. It sets the ground for seeing things as potentially dangerous and incriminating.

Judgment and Common Sense

This weaving of intentions, purposes, and clues is one element of common sense, which is not quite as mysterious as it sometimes seems. It means seeing contexts for what they are, seeing events and actions in them for what they are, knowing one's way about an activity, and having this skill in the usual areas of everyday life. Knowing one's way about is knowing how much weight to give to thoughts and actions—knowing how important they are, or knowing how seriously to take them. It is to grasp on the spot, prior to calculation (and preceding and grounding calculation), the

105

order in which things should occur, how likely it is that they will occur, and to which things one should pay attention. To know one's way about is to have judgment. It is to be able to grasp the usually likely and important, and to notice the actually likely and important, from among many possibilities. No merely technical knowledge can substitute for such judgment, which should govern its use.

One can judge incorrectly, of course. Moreover, because practical affairs involve persuading, convincing, and threatening, contexts and judgments can always shift. People hire Washington lobbyists because they know something is wrong with charts that show how bills become laws, and with pictures of neutral bureaucratic decisions. But they do not know what to do when, so they seek help: matters sometimes change quickly and unaccountably. We all know that friendship and threat are politically significant. But we need to activate them differentially and therefore unpredictably: their effect depends on charm, effort, one's own standing, and links to other events. Our usual grasp of the context for legislation and bureaucratic action enables us to see what we do not know, and to seek those with better judgment.

Unless we conserve practical, common-sensical knowledge of this sort we will fail politically. Such knowledge is available to those who have experience but not special technical competence. As the example of lobbying shows, however, we should direct narrow practical knowledge by a reasonable understanding of broader order and purpose. Indeed, to focus on fluid factors is often to forget the formal or ordered elements that set the political context: that these are the elected legislators (so, one's uncertainty about whom to lobby is not infinite), that these are the relevant agencies and committees (so, one need not talk with everyone), and that this is the form of the outcome one seeks (a law, bureaucratic rule, or executive decision). The formal elements of a context enable us to recognize and learn it.

The procedures we use to achieve success differ in different contexts. They are more or less subject to different choices (playing a piece's notes vs. composing it), open to cajoling, and different in scope and precision. These differences control how much we can teach practical knowledge and the degree to which effectiveness relies on experience. The more precisely the formal elements are arranged, and the more the purpose is absorbed in following proper forms, the more our actions are bound and predictable. Legislating would be easy if all that mattered were following correct procedures with no attention to useful results. Following religious rituals may seem to be the heart of piety, but rote observance may forget or stultify the natural activities they should sanctify. Yet, consider the injustice if everything were optional.

Linking Practical Activities

My discussion may seem to isolate practical activities from each other. But, in fact, they are usually linked. Common sense that works only within one context falls short of prudent understanding. Business, medicine, entertainment, and education do not go their own way simply, but work within a wider moral and legal arena. A clothing manufacturer is guided not just by his skill but by his customers' understanding of appropriate and beautiful use, and by how the community allows him to acquire and use resources.[13]

Because of the breadth of our freedom we sometimes overlook the place of the whole in directing and organizing our choices. Still, our constitutional order, our liberal democratic regime, is significant in forming us. It channels what we say and how we say it, so that we argue in terms of equality and individual rights. It is central in the character that we encourage—virtues such as responsibility that help us use our rights effectively. It is visible in the public opinion that guides our tastes and careers. And, it is crucial in choosing and enforcing measures that organize and restrict acquisition and choice.

Practical activities work within this larger context, or way of life. It gives us a sense of what others will do, how far they will go, what we may say to them, and how we ought to treat each other. It helps us judge in advance what to expect of others' actions and behavior, and how our ends interconnect. It also gives us an implicit grasp of the dangers and difficulties involved in our dealings, indicating, say, when we should use explicit contracts, when we can rely on people, and when their behavior is troublesome.

We can join these elements and suggest that an implicit trustworthiness and reputation exists among those with whom we deal. This trustworthiness involves expressing the expected virtues as we pursue ends that are structured and limited by equal rights. This broader trustworthiness informs the particular contexts of action.

Virtue and Practical Reason

The practical action and knowledge I am discussing are central to institutions and to our free way of life. They are vital in guiding and managing political affairs, although not sufficient for this. One way or another they shape and govern what is technical, and the realms of our happiness and success.

One may worry that practical knowledge and common sense are being overwhelmed, but we cannot simply lose them. The deeper concern should be to secure what is good in the purposes that form the contexts of practical action and to advance what is excellent in the virtues and judgment we use to operate within these contexts.[14] After all, trust may exist in poor institutions.

I will discuss this issue by exploring the link between liberal virtue and practical knowledge. I will concentrate on responsibility, as we see it in governing.

To responsibly do one's job requires the judgment that can secure success. This judgment sometimes means only that one knows what to do, does it, and honors one's agreements. In complex situations, however, such as political ones where we extend ourselves to wider spheres, responsible judgment often involves two related kinds of practical thinking connected to two dispositions and modes of action. These dispositions are compromise and enterprise. They become virtues for us, and effect just results, when the responsible, equal securing of rights directs them.

To be compromising is to follow the disposition to accept measures that settle differences about typical interests. It fits with the practical judgment by which we find these agreements and persuade others to agree to them. To be enterprising is to follow the disposition to transform interests in light of an end freshly understood or newly made salient. It fits with the judgment by which one projects the end and then convincingly works back from it in current terms until the new terms gain currency. Enterprise is primarily an executive and compromise primarily a legislative disposition and mode of action. In this sense, Ronald Reagan's anti–Soviet measures, born from the expectation that their regime was impermanent, and his reinvigorating of our economy by thinking unwaveringly in terms of private incentive and action, or Bill Clinton's and Newt Gingrich's transformation of welfare to see it more in terms of culture than income were enterprising. As with other just actions, however, they remained within the competitive, responsible, equal use of freedom in American life.

Compromising and enterprising thinking are not techniques. They are types of judgment under freedom's control. Their eye is on satisfying ends as part of securing liberty and the goods associated with it. They do not stipulate unbounded goals apart from the way of life that limits these goals. They shape and adjust more than they look and observe. Their thinking puts expertise and bureaucracy in their proper place.

From this viewpoint, to conserve liberty and virtue is also to try to secure the practical thinking connected to them, the continual fitting of things in place to advance equal freedom in the face of never-ending change, competition, and necessity. Some are more responsible and prudent than others, but practical action and thought are never matters of remote expertise beyond discussion and challenge. Of course, virtues do not assert themselves: we must assert them. The priority of character and practical thought to what is remote, impersonal, and bureaucratic makes evident their significance but does not guarantee their dominance.

Technology

Conservatives should fear the triumph of hyper-rationalism in the form of unchecked technology and technical thought, irrationalism in the form of theocratic extremism and the excesses of group identity, and intellectual complacency in the form of ignoring or misunderstanding liberty's rational grounding in natural rights. I have tried to steer between a conservatism too worried about theoretical abstraction to acknowledge the rational ground and prudent aspirations of natural rights and one too concerned about irrational restriction to see the coherence among individual rights, virtue, religion, and excellence properly understood. I now want more directly to discuss technology, whose revolutionary effects possibly threaten liberty, excellence, practical judgment, and virtue.

Concerns about technology's effects fit with many worries of traditional conservatism because rapid and cumulative change helps to overturn traditional ways. Technology is also coordinate with liberty, however, because liberating desires and discoveries follows from natural equality and open access to property.

We can normally deal with this tension practically. Contemporary science and technology, however, seem to present threats and opportunities that go beyond what we have come to expect, and, therefore, beyond the ways we have devised to control them. It seems that human abilities could be remarkably enhanced and human life spans remarkably extended. It appears, that is to say, that we are on the verge of creating ourselves. Has the project of liberty reached an end without measure, a point where human freedom may turn back upon itself to destroy humanity?

I will suggest four standpoints from which to guide us through this issue, practically and theoretically. First is that despite the appearance of novelty many issues that arise from today's technology are in fact similar to what we have dealt with recently. Responsibly controlling the environmental effects of industry or new weapons, for example, involves the same combination of prudence, political debate, and concern about security and the economy that we currently practice. Second is to remember that we deal with many effects of technology through still other technologies. Several scares about resource depletion during the past half-century were met with technologies that uncover newer resources and allow more extensive exploration. It is unwise to stifle the free use of talent for very long, subject to the prudent concerns about catastrophe, irreversibility, and security that normally guide regulation of science.

Third, and turning now more directly to what seems especially radical in our emerging powers over humanity, is to remember that our goal should be to protect the characteristics that allow us to make the best of ourselves. To conserve liberty and its associated virtues is to take this stance. Freedom and virtue speak to and from the reverence for what is inviolable in and beyond us. We protect this inviolability most visibly in what surrounds and sanctifies birth, marriage, and death. In the name of this inviolability we legally and customarily limit how we treat each other and what we permit. The restraints that govern us reflect our rational liberty and inviolability, but their ability to protect the inviolable seems also to require the ritual and reverence that grasps it implicitly and immediately. One consequence of decline in religious practice and faith is that the respect we have for each others' freedom and possible excellence may also decline. In any event, we need to subject technological development to the kind of respectful restraints we already honor.

Fourth, we cannot conserve our ability to choose the excellent unless we recognize it, and recognize the limits of what the nature of things allows us to do. To enhance qualities does not to tell us how to use them, in thought, art, and responsible attention to others and ourselves. It does not make visible the natural limits that we cannot overcome and that rebound upon us if we ignore them. It does not clarify what it is good to enhance. Even if, say, pleasure can in some sense be delivered with greater regularity and ease—as for a wealthy addict—its connection to different activities, to the mind's use in these activities, to the rank and complexity of these activities, to purity and satisfaction, are what they are and cannot change. The easily delivered pleasure will fall short of true pleasure. The experience of what is beautiful must always be an experience of what is radiant, fitting, and unique, something independent of us and not simply changeable by us. The attentive attachment required and permitted by love, the careful, patient, education of children may be affected by longer lives but cannot be altered fundamentally. The use of the mind to discover what is true cannot change what is true. We can distort but not eliminate our responsibility for our own liberty and self-government, for doing things for ourselves, and for thinking well enough of ourselves to protect what is good. We can warp our access to what is good but cannot alter what is good. The perfections beyond us are not subject to us. So, although regimes of liberty lead to remarkable change, the natural permanence of virtue, excellence, and freedom remain the guideposts for this change. If we are to preserve the excellent we must think about it carefully, protect the abilities that seek it, and not shy from demanding it.

Conclusion: Conservatism and the Future

Conservatism's future is secure if we allow ourselves to be awakened and reawakened by the permanent and not dazzled or frightened by the fleeting. Sensible conservatism looks back to what lasts. Our love of liberty is not a passing preference or odd quirk, but embraces a natural truth. Our defense of equal liberty does not stem from envy or guilt but from the attraction and substance of liberty itself. The character we need to secure our liberty is consistent with it, and encourages virtues that advance justified pride as well as economic interests, and that allow effective public action together with private interest. Our liberty and virtue permit us to recognize and choose ways of life and action that are naturally high, not only vulgar or narrow. Thoughtful return should also be the source of liberalism's regeneration, because its failures are most profoundly failures to understand.

The look back to our permanent ground is also the surest perspective from which to deal with our imperfections. We cannot perfectly enact our liberty, virtues, institutions, and self-governing, or make them altogether consistent. Still, a conservative disposition that intelligently recognizes such imperfection seeks in the last analysis to judge from the height on which liberty rests. We understand limits only in the light of aspirations.

NOTES

Introduction

1. I will use the terms liberal democracy, regimes of liberty, free regimes, conservative liberalism, and founding liberalism interchangeably to denote the form of government and way of life whose conservation I have in mind.

2. "If you analyze it, I believe that the very heart and soul of conservatism is libertarianism. I think conservatism is really a misnomer just as liberalism is a misnomer for the liberals—if we were back in the days of the Revolution, so-called conservatives today would be the Liberals and the liberals would be the Tories. The basis of conservatism is a desire for less government interference or less centralized authority or more individual freedom and this is a pretty general description also of what libertarianism is." Ronald Reagan, *Reason*, July 1, 1975.

3. One can find the message and budget at the Office of Management and Budget section of http://www.whitehouse.gov.

4. Walter Berns "The Perennial Trashing of Bourgeois Democracy," *Academic Questions*, vol. 15, no. 4 (September 2002): 23–26

5. Ross Douthat, "Theocracy, Theocracy, Theocracy," *First Things* 165 (August/September 2006): 23–30.

Chapter One

1. See http://www.aolnews.com.
2. See Alexis de Tocqueville, *Democracy in America*, vol. II, pt. IV, chap. 6. For Tocqueville generally see Harvey C. Mansfield, *Tocqueville: A Very Short Introduction* (Oxford University Press, 2010).
3. Consider Rousseau, *Discourse on the Origin of Inequality*, Burke, *Reflections on the Revolution in France*, Hegel, *Lectures on the Philosophy of History*, Marx, *Das Kapital*, Nietzsche, *Beyond Good and Evil*, and John Dewey, *The Public and its Problems*.
4. See the transcript of the Carter-Reagan debate of October 28, 1980, Commission on Presidential Debates (http://www.debates.org), and Reagan's addresses, "A Time for Choosing," (October 27, 1964), and "A Vision for America" (November 3, 1980), both in *President Ronald Reagan, The Quest for Peace, The Cause of Freedom*, The United States Information Agency, 1988.
5. Friedrich Nietzsche, *Beyond Good and Evil* (1886), sec. 9. Walter Kaufmann, trans. Vintage pb., 1966.
6. This is not to say that the moral and intellectual issues of enhancement as opposed to restoration are trivial.
7. Consider Mark Blitz, *Duty Bound* (Rowman and Littlefield, 2005), chap. 8.
8. Consider John Locke's discussion in his *Second Treatise of Government*.
9. Consider Locke's discussion in the *Second Treatise* and Hegel's in the *Philosophy of Right*.
10. For the question of nature and natural right generally consider Leo Strauss, *Natural Right and History* (University of Chicago Press, 1953).
11. I will develop these points in the next chapter.

Chapter Two

1. The value of volunteer time is based on the average hourly earnings of all production and non-supervisory workers on private non-farm payrolls (as determined by the Bureau of Labor Statistics). The Independent Sector takes this figure and increases it by 12% to estimate for fringe benefits. See the section of their website http://independentsector.org, "Value of Volunteer Time." They use

the Corporation for National and Community Service's report, *Volunteering in America: 2010* for their figures on the number of hours volunteered. The figure for philanthropic giving comes from the section of the Independent Sector's website, "The Sector's Economic Impact."

2. Practice HUMILITY, Franklin wisely tells us in the thirteenth of his "Thirteen Names of the Virtues." Humility's "precept" is: "Imitate Jesus and Socrates." Benjamin Franklin, *The Autobiography*, Part Two, page 1385 in The Library of America edition. See Deirdre McCloskey, *The Bourgeois Virtues* (University of Chicago Press, 2006).

3. See, for example, Nathan Tarcov, *Locke's Education for Liberty* (University of Chicago Press, 1984); William Galston, *Liberal Purposes* (Cambridge University Press, 1991); Stephen Macedo, *Liberal Virtues* (Oxford University Press, 1990); Peter Berkowitz, *Virtue and the Making of Modern Liberalism* (Princeton University Press, 1999); and McCloskey, *The Bourgeois Virtues.*

4. Consider, say, the life and character of George Washington, as discussed in Richard Brookhiser, *Founding Father* (Free Press, 1996) and Ron Chernow, *Washington* (The Penguin Press, 2010).

5. See Peter Wehner, "Civility and Double Standards," http://www. commentarymagazine.com/2011/02/21.

6. I will discuss practical reason in Chapter 4.

7. A good place to see the three virtues beginning to take root intellectually is in the work of John Locke, especially *A Letter Concerning Toleration* and *Some Thoughts Concerning Education.* See Berkowitz, *Virtue and the Making of Modern Liberalism.* Locke's *Thoughts* and other works provide material for the virtue of responsibility as I will discuss it, but do not name it. Consider, for that, *The Federalist.*

8. A useful place to start in examining many of these issues and the debates surrounding them is Brink Lindsey, *Paul Krugman's Nostalgianomics* (Cato Institute, 2009).

9. See *Federalist* 10.

10. Consider John Rawls, *A Theory of Justice* (Harvard University Press, 1971) and criticisms of his work such as David Schaefer, *Illiberal Justice* (University of Missouri Press, 2007).

11. Consider Locke's *Second Treatise*, chap. 6 (Paternal Power).

12. See Locke *Second Treatise*, 34.

13. See for this issue Plato's dialogue *Greater Hippias* 283C–286A, a discussion of law in Sparta.

Chapter Three

1. For these issues one should reflect on Tocqueville's *Democracy in America*, and Hegel's *Philosophy of Right*, among other works. Useful recent discussions in this vein include Hugh Heclo, *On Thinking Institutionally* (Paradigm Publishers, 2007); Kenneth Minogue, *The Servile Mind* (Encounter Books, 2010); Peter Lawler, *Modern and American Dignity* (Intercollegiate Studies Institute, 2010); and Daniel Mahoney, *The Conservative Foundations of the Liberal Order* (Intercollegiate Studies Institute, 2011).

2. Some of the writers who advance such views would object to being called liberals, but in the parlance of American politics they are on the left, sometimes the far left, hence "liberal." People with extreme versions of these views would stand outside the American consensus simply. To consider varieties of these positions one might read various works by Seyla Benhabib, Amitai Etzioni, Will Kymlicka, Michael Sandel, Charles Taylor, and Michael Walzer. See, for example, Michael Sandel, *Liberalism and the Limits of Justice* (Cambridge University Press, 1982), and Michael Walzer, *Politics and Passion* (Yale University Press, 2006).

3. See several of the essays in Ingrid Creppell, Russel Hardin, and Stephen Macedo, eds. *Toleration on Trial* (Lexington Books, 2008). One should also consider Prime Minister David Cameron's speech on Islamist extremism at the Munich Security Conference, February 5, 2011, the text of which can be found on http://www.number10.gov.uk.

4. One should consider for this issue Michael Novak, *The Spirit of Democratic Capitalism* (Simon and Schuster, 1982) and Peter Berger, *The Capitalist Revolution* (Basic Books, 1986). For the overall question of capitalism and its limits see Irving Kristol, *Two Cheers for Capitalism* (Basic Books, 1978).

5. Consider here Tocqueville, *Democracy in America*, vol. I, pt. I, chap. 9.

6. One can find this information in easily available Gallup, Fox News, and other polls, and in a major survey (The US Religious Landscape Survey) conducted in 2007 by the Pew Forum on Religion and Public Life. In the same Pew survey in which 92% said they believe in God, however, only 39% said they attended religious services at least once a week. The survey was "based on interviews with more than 35,000 American adults," and is available at http://religions.pewforum.org.

7. Consider James W. Ceaser, *Reconstructing America* (Yale University Press, 2000), and "A Genealogy of Anti-Americanism," *The Public Interest*, Summer, 2003.

8. Consider Bach and Mozart's music, Shakespeare's plays and Greek comedy and tragedy, Strauss's waltzes and Gilbert and Sullivan operas, and Liszt's and Paganini's popularity.

9. For these issues generally consider various works by Tyler Cowen, including *In Praise of Commercial Culture* (Harvard University Press, 2000), and *Creative Destruction* (Princeton University Press, 2004).

Chapter Four

1. Consider Tocqueville's discussion of these matters in *Democracy in America*.

2. Gallup Poll approval ratings for the 111th Congress, for example, averaged 25%, among the lowest in the past two decades. The December 2010 rating was 13%, the lowest ever, before rising to 20% in January 2011

3. One might consider the statements of the "No Labels" movement that arose late in 2010 and the views of many of its organizers, and EJ Dionne's book *Why Americans Hate Politics* (Simon and Schuster, 1992), together with many of his subsequent columns in *The Washington Post.*

4. For a discussion of formal mechanisms that might limit the sway of self-identified liberals and conservatives and advance the fortunes both of self-identified moderates and (the authors argue) the Democratic Party, see William A. Galston and Elaine C. Kamarck, "The Still Vital Center," a report from the think tank Third Way, February, 2011.

5. We see something similar among those who nostalgically favor a pretty picture of communal brotherhood and push to the side the tyranny of elders who repress those who wish to be individually free.

6. Consider the debates about air power, tank warfare, and offensive and defensive weaponry between the first and second world wars and the current discussions of the proper structure and size of U.S. forces. Small groups of officers rather than central military planners were often correct, and informed statesmen sometimes but not always knew more than many in the military. Here as in other areas one could usefully study Churchill and DeGaulle's words and actions.

7. Subsidiarity is a Catholic social teaching that we should deal with affairs at the lowest, least centralized, level of authority.

8. Consider the question of slavery and segregation in the United States.

9. For the question of families and localities consider Edward Banfield, *The Moral Basis of a Backward Society* (The Free Press, 1958).

10. Or, they may fail to do so, but they are still a venue for appeal.

11. This section draws on Mark Blitz, "The Common Sense of Practical Knowledge," *Journal of Law and Economic Policy*, vol. 4, no. 1 (Fall 2007), pp 177–189.

12. "The same thought can, in an other place, have a whole other worth." Lessing, *Leibniz, von den ewigen Strafen*.

13. Aristotle's *Politics* and Plato's *Statesman* and *Republic* express these links most clearly. As they see it, the founders of the community's way of life, its legislators, ultimately validate and permit its ends and means. They form many activities into a whole. Resources are at the beck and call of the community in war, and actions need to observe rules of use, possession, and distribution.

14. This securing, as I am suggesting, requires some explicit and even theoretical understanding of our rights, virtues, goals, and self-governing.

BIBLIOGRAPHY

Aristotle. *Nicomachean Ethics*. Translation, glossary, and introductory essay by Joe Sachs. Newburyport, MA: Focus Publishing, 2003.
———. *The Politics*. Translated and with introduction, notes, and glossary by Carnes Lord. Chicago: The University of Chicago Press, 1984.

Banfield, Edward, C. *The Moral Basis of a Backward Society*. New York: The Free Press, 1958.

Berger, Peter. *The Capitalist Revolution*. New York: Basic Books, 1986.

Berkowitz, Peter. *Virtue and the Making of Modern Liberalism*. Princeton: Princeton University Press, 1999.

Berns, Walter. "The Perennial Trashing of Bourgeois Democracy." *Academic Questions*, 15 (2002): 23–26.

Blitz, Mark. "The Common Sense of Practical Knowledge." *Journal of Law and Economic Policy* 4 (2007): 177–189.
———. *Duty Bound: Responsibility and American Public Life*. Lanham, MD: Rowman and Littlefield, 2005.

Brookhiser, Richard. *Founding Father: Rediscovering George Washington*. New York: The Free Press, 1996.

Burke, Edmund. *Reflections on the Revolution in France*. Edited by Frank M. Turner. New Haven: Yale University Press, 2003.

Cameron, David. Speech at the Munich Security Conference, February 5, 2011. http://www.number10.gov.uk/.

Ceaser, James W. "A Genealogy of Anti-Americanism." *The Public Interest*, Summer, 2003.

———. *Reconstructing America*. New Haven: Yale University Press, 2000.

Chernow, Ron. *Washington: A Life*. New York, London: Penguin Press, 2010.

Cowen, Tyler. *Creative Destruction*. Princeton: Princeton University Press, 2004.

———. *In Praise of Commercial Culture*. Cambridge, MA: Harvard University Press, 2000.

Creppell, Ingrid, and Russell Hardin, and Stephen Macedo, eds. *Toleration on Trial*. Lanham, MD: Lexington Books, 2008.

Dewey, John. *The Public and its Problems*. Chicago: Swallow Press, 1954.

Dionne, E. J. *Why Americans Hate Politics*. New York: Simon and Schuster, 1992.

Douthat, Ross. "Theocracy, Theocracy, Theocracy." *First Things* 165 (2006): 23–30.

Franklin, Benjamin. *Writings*. New York: Library of America, 1987.

Galston, William. *Liberal Purposes*. Cambridge: Cambridge University Press, 1991.

———. William A. and Elaine C. Kamarck, "The Still Vital Center." Third Way. February, 2011. http://www.thirdway.org/.

Hamilton, Alexander, and James Madison and John Jay. *The Federalist Papers*. Edited by Clinton Rossiter. Introduction and notes by Charles R. Kesler. New York: Signet Classics, 2003.

Heclo, Hugh. *On Thinking Institutionally*. Boulder, CO: Paradigm Publishers, 2007.

Hegel, Georg Wilhelm Friedrich. *Elements of the Philosophy of Right*. Edited by Allen W. Wood. Translated by H. B. Nisbet. Cambridge: Cambridge University Press, 1991.

———. *Lectures on the Philosophy of World History*. Translated by H. B. Nisbet. Cambridge: Cambridge University Press, 1975.

Independent Sector. *Volunteering in America: 2010*. Last updated 2011. http://www.independentsector.org/volunteer_time.

Kristol, Irving. *Two Cheers for Capitalism*. New York: Basic Books, 1978.

Lawler, Peter. *Modern and American Dignity*. Intercollegiate Studies Institute, 2010.

Lessing, Gotthold Ephraim. *Philosophical and Theological Writings.* Translated by H. B. Nisbet. Cambridge: Cambridge University Press, 2005.

Lindsey, Brink. *Paul Krugman's Nostalgianomics.* Cato Institute, 2009.

Locke, John. *Some Thoughts Concerning Education and Of the Conduct of the Understanding.* Edited by Ruth W. Grant and Nathan Tarcov. Indianapolis: Hackett, 1996.

———. *Two Treatises of Government and A Letter Concerning Toleration.* Edited by Ian Shapiro. New Haven: Yale University Press, 2003.

Macedo, Stephen. *Liberal Virtues.* Oxford: Oxford University Press, 1990.

Mahoney, Daniel. *The Conservative Foundations of the Liberal Order.* Intercollegiate Studies Institute, 2011.

Mansfield, Harvey C. *Tocqueville: A Very Short Introduction.* Oxford: Oxford University Press, 2010.

Marx, Karl. *Capital.* Translated by Samuel Moore and Edward Aveling. New York: International Publishers, 1967.

McCloskey, Deirdre. *The Bourgeois Virtues.* Chicago: University of Chicago Press, 2006.

Minogue, Kenneth. *The Servile Mind: How Democracy Erodes the Moral Life.* New York: Encounter Books, 2010.

Nietzsche, Friedrich. *Beyond Good and Evil: Prelude to a Philosophy of the Future.* Translated with commentary by Walter Kaufmann. New York: Vintage Books, 1966.

Novak, Michael. *The Spirit of Democratic Capitalism.* New York: Simon and Schuster, 1982.

Obama, Barack. "Presidential Transmittal Letter Budget FY 2010." May 2009. http://www.whitehouse.gov/omb/omb/Message.

Pelosi, Nancy. "House Floor Speech on Health Care Reform Bill." March 21, 2010.

Plato. *Greater Hippias. The Roots of Political Philosophy: Ten Forgotten Socratic Dialogues.* Translated, with interpretive studies. Edited by Thomas L. Pangle. Ithaca: Cornell University Press, 1987.

———. *Republic. Plato's Republic.* Translated, with notes and an interpretive essay by Allan Bloom. New York: Basic Books, 1968.

———. *Statesman. Plato's Statesman.* Translated and with commentary by Seth Benardete. Chicago: University of Chicago Press, 1996.

Rawls, John. *A Theory of Justice.* Cambridge, MA: Harvard University Press, 1971.

Reagan, Ronald. Interview. *Reason.* July (1975).

———. *The Quest for Peace, the Cause of Freedom: Selected Speeches on the United States and the World.* Washington, D.C.: The United States Information Agency, 1988.

Rousseau, Jean Jacques. *The Discourses and other early political writings.* Edited by Victor Gourevitch. Cambridge: Cambridge University Press, 1997.

Sandel, Michael. *Liberalism and the Limits of Justice.* Cambridge: Cambridge University Press, 1982.

Schaefer, David. *Illiberal Justice: John Rawls vs. The American Political Tradition.* Columbia and London: University of Missouri Press, 2007.

Strauss, Leo. *Natural Right and History.* Chicago: University of Chicago Press, 1953.

Tarcov, Nathan. *Locke's Education for Liberty.* Chicago: University of Chicago Press, 1984.

Tocqueville, Alexis de. *Democracy in America.* Translated, edited, and with an introduction by Harvey C. Mansfield and Delba Winthrop. Chicago: University of Chicago Press, 2000.

Walzer, Michael. *Politics and Passion: Toward a More Egalitarian Liberalism.* New Haven: Yale University Press, 2006.

Wehner, Peter. "Civility and Double Standards." http://www.commentary magazine.com/2011/02/21/civility-and-double-standards/.

ABOUT THE AUTHOR

Mark Blitz (AB and PhD from Harvard University) is the Fletcher Jones Professor of Political Philosophy and director of the Henry Salvatori Center at Claremont McKenna College. He served during the Reagan administration as associate director of the United States Information Agency. He has been vice president of the Hudson Institute and has taught political theory at Harvard University and at the University of Pennsylvania. He is the author of *Plato's Political Philosophy; Duty Bound: Responsibility and American Public Life;* and *Heidegger's "Being and Time" and the Possibility of Political Philosophy* and is coeditor (with William Kristol) of *Educating the Prince.*

BOYD AND JILL SMITH TASK FORCE ON VIRTUES OF A FREE SOCIETY

The Boyd and Jill Smith Task Force on Virtues of a Free Society examines the evolution of America's core values, how they are threatened, and what can be done to preserve them. The task force's aims are to identify the enduring virtues and values on which liberty depends; chart the changes in how Americans have practiced virtues and values over the course of our nation's history; assess the ability of contemporary associations and institutions—particularly schools, family, and religion—to sustain the necessary virtues; and discuss how society might nurture the virtues and values on which its liberty depends.

The core membership of this task force includes Peter Berkowitz, David Brady, Gerard V. Bradley, James W. Ceaser, William Damon, Robert P. George, Tod Lindberg, Harvey C. Mansfield, Russell Muirhead, Clifford Orwin, and Diana Schaub.

INDEX